The Indian Wars Volunteer

The Indian Wars Volunteer

Recollections of the Conflict Against
the Snakes, Shoshone, Bannocks,
Modocs and Other Native Tribes
of the American North West

William Thompson

LEONAUR

The Indian Wars Volunteer: Recollections of the Conflict Against the Snakes,
Shoshone, Bannocks, Modocs and Other Native Tribes of the American North West
by William Thompson

First published under the title
Reminiscences of a Pioneer

Leonaur is an imprint of Oakpast Ltd

ISBN: 978-1-84677-544-4 (hardcover)
ISBN: 978-1-84677-543-7 (softcover)

http://www.leonaur.com

Publisher's Notes

The opinions expressed in this book are those of the author
and are not necessarily those of the publisher.

Contents

Foreword 7

Wagon's West 9

Oregon 18

The Indian Outbreak of 1855 25

I Shoot My Indian 35

Taking Revenge on Marauding Snakes 51

Death of the Shoshone Chief 61

My Pistol Gunfight 71

Depredations of the Modoc Indians 76

The Ben Wright Massacre 80

Treaty With the Modocs is Made 83

Battle in the Lava Beds 92

The Peace Commission's Work 105

Three Days' Battle in the Lava Beds 111

Trailing the Fugitives 119

The Great Bannock War 126

Snake Uprising in Eastern Oregon 137

Bannocks Double on their Tracks 142

Another Attack that Miscarried 151

Reign of the Vigilantes 158

The Passing of the Mogans 166

The Lookout Lynching 169

Conclusion 177

Foreword

So rapidly is the Far West changing character, our pioneers should feel in duty bound to preserve all they can of its early history. Many of them are giving relics of frontier days to museums and historical societies. And they do well. Yet such collections are unfortunately accessible to only the few. Hence they do better who preserve the living narratives of their times. For however unpretentious from the cold aspect of literary art, these narratives breathe of courage and fortitude amid hardships and perils, and tell as nothing else can of the hopes and dreams of the hardy pathfinders, and of the compensations and pleasures found in their sacrifices.

It is with this end in view, to preserve the life of the old days in its many colours, that these recollections are penned. There was more to this life than has been touched by the parlour romancers or makers of moving-picture films. Perhaps someday these memories may serve to illumine the historian delving in the human records of the past. And perhaps, also, and this is the author's dearest wish, they may inspire young readers to hold to the hardy traditions of the 'Fifties and to keep this spirit alive in a country destined soon to be densely peopled with newcomers from the long-settled parts of the world.

CHAPTER 1

Wagon's West

I have often wondered, when viewing a modern passenger coach, with its palace cars, its sleeping and dining cars, if those who cross the "Great American Desert," from the Mississippi to the Pacific in four days, realize the hardships, dangers and privations of the Argonauts of fifty-eight years ago. The "Plains" were then an unbroken wilderness of three thousand miles, inhabited by hordes of wild Indians, and not too friendly to the white man journeying through his country.

The trip then required careful preparation—oxen, wagons, provisions, arms and ammunition must be first of all provided. These were essentials, and woe to the hapless immigrant who neglected these provisions. To be stranded a thousand miles from the "settlements" was a fate none but the most improvident and reckless cared to hazard.

It is to recount some of the trials, adventures, hardships, privations, as I remember them, that these lines are written. For truly, the immigrants of the early 50s were the true "Conquerors of the Wilderness." Cutting loose from home and civilization, their all, including their women and children, loaded into wagons, and drawn by slow-moving ox teams, they fearlessly braved three thousand miles of almost trackless wilderness.

As a small boy I remember the first mention of California, the land of gold. My father returned from New Orleans in January. On board the steamer coming up the Mississippi river, he had fallen in with some gentlemen "returning to the States." They had given him a glowing description of the "land of gold," and almost the first words spoken after the family greetings were over was, "We are going to California in the spring."

My mother was more than agreeable and from that time nothing was talked or thought of but the journey to California. The old refrain was sung from morning to night:

In the spring we're going to journey,
Far away to California.

My chum, Tant, a negro boy of my own age, and I seriously discussed the prospects and dangers of the journey. Direful tales of the tomahawk and scalping knife were recounted by the older children. But Tant's fears were allayed by the assurance that the "Injuns" would not kill and scalp a black boy with a woolly head. For once in my life I envied that imp of darkness.

In February a gentleman came to our home and after dinner he and my father rode over the plantation. The next morning they rode over to Bolliver, the county seat. Returning in the evening my father announced that the plantation was sold. Then began the real preparations for the journey. My father was constantly in the saddle. Oxen, wagons, ox yokes, ox bows, cattle, covers for wagons, arms, ammunition and provisions were purchased and brought to the plantation. All was hurry and excitement. Two shoemakers came to our home to make up the leather purchased at St. Louis or from neighbouring tanneries. Meantime Aunt Ann and the older girls of the family were busy spinning and weaving. Every article of wearing apparel must be made at home. "Store clothes" were out of the question in those days. Wool must be carded and spun into thread for Aunt Ann's old wooden loom. The cloth was then fashioned into garments for clothing to last a year after we should reach our goal far out on the Pacific shores. The clank of the old wooden loom was almost ceaseless. Merrily the shuttle sang to an accompaniment of a camp meeting melody. Neighbours also kindly volunteered their services in weaving and fashioning garments for the family. All was bustle and hurry.

At last all was in readiness for the start. Spring with all its beauty and glory was with us, and friends from the country round and about had come to bid us a final farewell—friends, alas, we were destined never to meet again. The parting I remember as the first real sorrow of a life that has experienced most of the hardships, dangers, privations and sufferings of a wild frontier life. It was a beautiful morning early in April, 1852, that the leaders were pointed to the west and a start was made. Four wagons were drawn by five yoke of oxen each, while the fifth, the family wagon, was drawn by three yoke.

The first weeks of our journey were passed without anything happening worthy of note. At Caw river we were detained several days by high water. Here we began falling in with others, who, like, ourselves, were bound for the golden shores of the Pacific. And it was here that we made the acquaintance of families, and friendships formed that were to survive not only the privations of the plains but were to last a life time. Men were drawn together on the plains as in the everyday walks of life, only the bonds were closer and far more enduring. The very dangers through which they passed together rendered the ties more lasting. "Our train" henceforth consisted of my father's, Littleton Younger, John Gant, "Uncle" Johnny Thompson and a party of five Welsh gentlemen, under the leadership of a gentleman named Fathergill, and a prince of a gentleman he was. At that time there was not a cabin in what is now the great and populous State of Kansas. Only vast undulating plains, waving with grass, traversed here and there with timber-skirted streams. Game was abundant, consisting mostly of antelope and prairie chickens. Our Welsh friends, being bachelors and having no loose stock, were the hunters for the train, and supplied us with an abundance of fresh meat.

As we proceeded westward more immigrants were met, and often our camp resembled a tented city. All was then a pleasure trip—a picnic, as it were. No sooner was camp struck than a place was cleared and dancing began to the sound of the violin. Many of these young ladies were well dressed—actually wore "store clothes!" But alas, and alack, I was destined to see these same young ladies who started out so gay and care-free, in tattered dresses, barefooted and dusty, walking and driving the loose cattle. Too many excursions and pleasure jaunts had reduced their horses to skeletons before the real trials of the journey had fairly begun. But the women of '52 and '53 were not of the namby-pamby sort. When the trials came they were brave and faced privations and dangers with the same fortitude as their stronger brothers.

At Fort Laramie we crossed the Platte river by fording. The stream, as I remember it, was near a mile wide, but not waist deep. Thirty and forty oxen were hitched to one wagon, to effect the crossing. But woe to the hapless team that stalled in the treacherous quicksands. They must be kept going, as it required but a short stop for the treacherous sands to engulf team and wagon alike. Men wading on either side of the string of oxen kept them moving, and soon all were safely on the north side of the Platte river.

We soon began to see great herds of buffalo. In fact, at times the hills were black with the heaving, rolling, bellowing mass, and no meal was served for many days without fresh buffalo. As we wended our way up the valley of the Platte one could look back for miles and miles on a line of wagons, the sinuous line with varicoloured wagon covers resembling a great serpent crawling and wriggling up the valley. Fortunately for "our train" we were well in advance and thus escaped the sickness that later dotted the valley of the Platte with graves.

On and on. Independence Rock, Sweet Water, and Devil's Gate were passed. Members of our train had observed two men who travelled with us, yet held themselves aloof.

They appeared to prefer their own company, and while they travelled along with us, probably for protection, they always camped by themselves. Some said they were Mormons, while others asserted they were merely a selfish pair. One day one of the men was missing. The other on being questioned gave evasive and very unsatisfactory replies. His actions excited the suspicions of our men. He appeared anxious to get ahead and left us, making a long night drive. It was then determined to make an investigation. Two of our party mounted good horses and started back on the trail. Each camp was carefully examined until they were rewarded by finding the body of a murdered man beneath the ashes of a camp fire, buried in a shallow grave. By riding all night they overtook the train, before starting back burying the body of the unfortunate traveller. The news spread rapidly and a party followed the murderer. He was soon overtaken and halted at the muzzles of rifles. When the train came up a council was held. Probably a hundred wagons were halted. It was determined to give the man a trial. The evidence was conclusive, and after conviction the miserable wretch confessed all, but begged for mercy. He said the murdered man had picked him up out of pity and was taking him through for his company and his help. There being no trees, three wagons were run together, the wagon tongues being raised to form a tripod and to answer for a gallows. To the centre of the tripod a rope was attached with the other end around the neck of the trembling, writhing, begging wretch. But he had committed a cruel, cold-blooded murder and his crime could not be condoned. He was stood on the back of a horse, and a sharp cut being given the animal the wretch was swung into eternity. A grave had been dug and into this the body of the murderer was placed. The property of the murdered man was taken through to the settlements. His relatives were communicated with, the property sold and the proceeds sent to the proper owners. Such was the swift but terrible justice administered on the plains. Without law or officers of the law, there was no other course to pursue consistent with safety to the living.

July 4th, 1852, we reached Green river. Traders had established six ferry boats at the crossing. In order to keep down competition, five of the boats were tied up and the sum of $18 was demanded for each and every wagon ferried over the stream. They had formed a kind of "trust," as it were, even in that day. The rate was pronounced exorbitant, unfair, outrageous, and beyond the ability of many to pay. Train after train had been blocked until a city of tents had been formed. On the morning of the 4th a meeting of immigrants was called to discuss the situation. A few counselled moderation, compromise, anything to prevent a clash with the traders, who boasted that they could turn the Indians loose on us. The great majority defied both traders and Indians and boldly announced that they would fight before they would submit to being robbed. Many fiery speeches were made, and about 10 o'clock a long line of men, with shouldered rifles flashing in the sun, marched down and took possession of the ferry boats. The traders fumed and threatened, and Indians with war-whoops and yells mounted horses and rode off from the opposite side. The traders said they were going after the tribe to exterminate the entire train. They were plainly told that the first shot fired by traders or Indians would sound their own death knell—that they, the traders, would be shot down without mercy.

The ferry boats were then seized and the work of crossing the river began. As fast as the wagons were crossed over they were driven down the river, one behind another, forming a corral, with the open side facing the river in the form of a half wheel. When the wagons had all been crossed, the loose stock was swum over into the opening. There was no confusion, but everything proceeded with almost military precision. A committee had been appointed to keep tally on the number of wagons crossed on the boats. The traders were then paid

$4 for each and every wagon. Still they fumed and threatened. The faces of the more timid blanched and a few women were in tears. I beheld the whole proceedings with childish wonder. But the circumstances of that 4th of July and the execution of the murderer were burned into my brain with letters of fire, never to be effaced while memory holds her sway.

Every man was under arms that night. Horses were tied up and the work oxen chained to the wagons, a strict guard being kept on the traders in the mean time. The next morning the long string of wagons started out on the road. Two hundred men rode on either side to defend the train, while scouting parties rode at a distance to guard against surprise. This formation was kept up for several days, but seeing neither traders nor Indians the different trains separated and each went its way unmolested.

Bear river and Soda Springs were next passed. A few miles this side of Soda Springs the roads forked, one going to California and the other to Oregon. Here a council was held. A portion of "our train" wanted to take the California road. Others preferred the Oregon route. A vote was taken and resulted in a majority for Oregon, and association and friendship being stronger than mere individual preference, all moved out on the Oregon road.

Snake River was finally reached, and here the real trials of the journey began. From some cause, not then understood, our oxen began to die. The best and fattest died first, often two and three in one camp. Cows were drawn into the yoke and the journey resumed. But it soon became evident that loads must be lightened. Wagons loaded with stores and provisions were driven to the side of the road and an invitation written with charcoal for all to help themselves. To add to the difficulties of our situation, the Snake Indians were surly and insolent to a degree. Gradually a gloom settled over all. No more of laughter, of dancing and song. And faster and faster the oxen died. Camping places were almost unbearable on account of the dead and decaying cattle. And then the terrible mountains of which we had heard so much were before us. Would we ever reach the settlements? This was a question that began to prey upon the minds of many. A few of the young men shouldered a blanket and some provisions and started on foot to reach the valley. Others began to despair of ever reaching the promised land. If those who cross the continent now in palace cars and complain of the tediousness of the journey could take one look at the wreck and desolation that lined the poisoned banks of Snake River, they would hide their heads in very shame.

As our situation became more desperate it appeared the Indians became more sullen and mean. Guards were kept night and day, the women and children driving the teams and loose cattle and horses in order that the men might get some rest. At one point the danger seemed imminent. The men on night guard reported that the horses were snorting and acting as if Indians were about. Mr. Fathergill's mule appeared especially uneasy. The cattle and horses were then all driven to camp, the horses tied up and the oxen chained to the wagons. The next morning moccasin tracks were discovered within a hundred yards of our camp, showing plainly that only extreme caution and foresight had saved us all from massacre. After that camps were selected with a view to defence. A point was finally reached where we were to bid farewell to the dread Snake River. Several trains camped there that night. Among them was a man named Wilson, a brother of ex-Senator Henry Wilson of Colusa county. Cattle had been rounded up and oxen placed under the yoke. Wilson became involved in a quarrel with a young man in his employ. Suddenly both drew revolvers and began firing at each other. The duel ended by Wilson falling from his mule, a dead man. The young man rode away and was seen no more. A grave was dug, the dead man buried and within two hours the train was in motion. There was no time for tears or ceremonies. Winter was coming on, and the terrible mountains must be crossed. Besides the dread of an Indian attack was ever present.

After leaving Snake River we lost no more cattle. We crossed the Blue Mountains without any mishap. We met several settlers coming out with teams to help any that might be in distress. They were told to go on back, as others were behind far more in need of assistance than we. On reaching the Columbia river we found the Indians very friendly and obtained an abundance of fresh salmon. Trifles were traded for salmon and wild currants, which formed a welcome addition to our bill of fare. The dreaded Cascade Mountains were finally reached. A storm was raging on the mountain and we were advised by settlers whom we met coming out to assist the immigrants, to wait for better weather. Some disregarded the advice and paid dearly for their temerity, losing many of their cattle, and only for the help rendered by the settlers might themselves have perished.

As soon as the storm spent its force a start was made and the dreaded mountains passed in six days, and without any serious mishap. On reaching the valley we were everywhere greeted with genuine western hospitality. Vegetables were plentiful and cheap—in fact could be had for the asking. But while wheat was abundant there were no mills to grind it into flour, and we soon discovered that that very necessary article could not be had for love or money. We were therefore soon reduced to a daily diet of boiled wheat, potatoes, pumpkins and wild meat, the latter requiring but little exertion to secure. But we were as well off as anybody else, and with the remnants of clothing saved from the wreck of the desert and plains passed the winter in health and some degree of comfort.

CHAPTER 2

Oregon

The winter of 1852-53 will forever be memorable in the annals of pioneer days in Oregon. Indeed, nothing comparable had been experienced by immigrants in former years. Deep snows encompassed us from without, and while we were sheltered from the storms by a comfortable log cabin, and were supplied with a fair amount of provisions such as they were, a gloom settled over all. Cattle and horses were without forage and none could be had. Reduced to skin and bone by the long and toilsome journey across the plains, they were illy prepared to stand the rigors of such a winter. In this extremity recourse was had to the forest. The Oregon woods, as all are aware, are covered by long streamers of yellow moss, and in the cutting of firewood it was discovered this moss was devoured with a relish by cattle and horses.

Then began the struggle to save our stock. From early morning to night the ring of the axe was unceasing. The cattle, especially, soon learned the meaning of the cracking of a tree and bolted for the spot. To prevent them being killed by the falling trees, the smaller children were pressed into service to herd them away until the tree was on the ground. The stock soon began to thrive and cows gave an increased amount of milk which was hailed with delight by the small children and afforded a welcome addition to their bill of fare—boiled wheat, potatoes, meat, and turnips.

Thus wore away the terrible winter of 1852-53. I say terrible, and the word but poorly expresses our situation during that memorable winter. To fully understand our situation one has but to imagine oneself in a strange land, far from human aid, save from those environed as ourselves. We were three thousand miles from "home," surrounded by a primeval wilderness, in which ever lurked the treacherous savage. Happily for us and for all, no annoyance or real danger threatened us from that quarter. A few years before, a salutary lesson had been taught the savages. The deadly rifles of the pioneers had instilled into their bosoms a wholesome fear. Information had reached the settlers that the Indians contemplated a massacre—that they were going to break out. The information reached them through the medium of a friendly Indian. The result was that the settlers "broke out" first. A company was formed, consisting of about all of the able-bodied men within reach. The savages were encountered on the Molalley and after a sharp fight were dispersed or killed. Several were left dead on the ground. The whites had one man wounded. Thus the war power of the Molalleys was destroyed forever.

In this connection I wish to make a digression, which I trust my readers will pardon. It has often been urged that the white man has shown little gratitude and no pity for the aborigines of this country. This I wish to refute. The Indian that brought the word of warning to the white settlers was ever after the object of tender solicitude on the part of those whom he had befriended. I have seen that Indian, then old and possibly worse off for his association with civilization, sitting down and bossing a gang of Chinamen cutting and splitting wood for Dan'l Waldo. The Indian, "Quinaby," always contracted the sawing of the wood at $2.00 per cord and hired the Chinamen to do the work for 50 cents per cord. He had a monopoly on the wood-sawing business for Mr. Waldo, Wesley Shannon, and other old pioneers. It mattered not to "Quinaby" that prices went down, his contract price remained the same, and the old pioneers heartily enjoyed the joke, and delighted in telling it on themselves.

But enough of this. Spring came at last and a new world burst upon the vision of the heretofore almost beleaguered pioneers. We had wintered on a "claim" belonging to a young man named John McKinney, two miles from the present town of Jefferson. He had offered his cabin as a shelter with true Western hospitality, including the free use of land to plant a crop. Accordingly about twenty acres were ploughed and sown to wheat. This work was performed by my elder brothers. Meantime my father had started out to look for a claim. Nine miles north of Eugene City he purchased a "claim" of 320 acres, paying therefore an Indian pony and $40 in cash. To this place we moved early in May, and there began the task of building up a home in the western wilds. A small cabin of unhewn logs constituted the only improvement on the "claim," but a new house of hewn logs was soon erected and a forty-acre field enclosed with split rails. We had plenty of neighbours who, like ourselves, were improving their lands, and mutual assistance was the rule.

As summer approached it became necessary to return to our wintering place, where a crop had been sown, and harvest the same. Accordingly, my father, accompanied by my two older brothers, the late Judge J. M. Thompson of Lane County, and Senator S. C. Thompson, Jr., of Wasco, then boys of 12 and 14 years, went back and cared for the grain. The wheat was cut with a cradle, bound into bundles and stacked. A piece of ground was then cleared, the grain laid down on the "tramping floor" and oxen driven around until the grain was all tramped out. After the grain was all "threshed out," it was carried on top of a platform built of rails and poured out on a wagon sheet, trusting to the wind to separate the wheat kernels from the straw and chaff. By this primitive method the crop was harvested, threshed, cleaned, and then sacked. It was then hauled by ox teams to Albany where a small burr mill had been erected by a man named Monteith, if my memory serves me correctly, and then ground to flour.

And then, joy of joys! We had wheat bread. No more boiled wheat, nor flour ground in a coffee mill,—but genuine wheat bread. You, reader, who probably never ate a meal in your life without bread, have little conception of the deliciousness of a biscuit after the lapse of a year. As Captain Applegate once said to the writer, referring to the first wheat bread he ever remembered eating: "No delicacy,—no morsel of food ever eaten in after life tasted half so delicious as that bread." It must be remembered that Captain Applegate crossed the plains in 1843 and was therefore an "old settler" when we arrived. His trials were prolonged only a matter of eight years; but looking back, what an eternity was encompassed in those eight years.

One of the leading characteristics of the Anglo-Saxon is that on coming to the western hemisphere he brought with him his wife and children,— his school books, and his Bible. As soon, therefore, as a spot for a home had been selected and a rude shelter of logs erected for loved ones, the neighbours began discussing the question of school. It was finally arranged that we must have a school, and the cabin of a bachelor settler was tendered and accepted, and my father chosen as teacher. Logs were split open and placed on legs, with the flat sides turned up to serve as seats. The floor,—well, Mother Earth provided that. It was sprinkled and swept out with "split brooms" twice daily. To prevent the pupils getting lost in the tall grass of the prairies, furrows were ploughed from the settlers' cabins to the school house. This also served as a protection to the barefoot girls and boys going to and from, school. My father belonged to the old school and did not believe in "sparing the rod," and as a result, it became indelibly impressed upon my juvenile mind that he used the rod upon me to better preserve order among the other pupils.

In those days girls dressed in "linsey woolsey," while the boys of all ages wore buckskin pantaloons and hickory shirts. Now, buckskin is well calculated to stand the wear and tear of even a robust boy. Yet there were awkward drawbacks. The legs of the pantaloons absorbed too much moisture from the dew-bedecked grass and they would stretch out to almost any length. The boy, therefore, must roll them up at the bottom. Arrived at school, however, the drying process set in, and he, perforce, must unroll the legs. As the boy occupied a sitting position, the legs of his buckskins set to the crook of his knees. Imagine, if you will, a row of boys ranging from 12 to 17 years, standing in a class reciting their lessons, straight as hickories, yet the pantaloons of every mother's son of them still sitting down. But it mattered little to the boy of that day, as he had only to wet them again, stretch them out straight and wear them to "meetin' in the grove" Sunday.

There was no aristocracy—no "four hundred"—in those primitive days. All dressed alike, ate the same kind of food, and every man, woman, and child was as good as every other man, woman, and child, provided they were honest, kind neighbours, ready and willing to render assistance in sickness or in need. In fine, these pioneers constituted a pure democracy, where law was the simple rule of honesty, friendship, mutual help, and good will, where "duty was love and love was law."

One must not imagine that life was wholly devoid of pleasures in those days. The young of both sexes always rode horseback, whether to church in the grove, or going the round of parties, candy pullings, or kissing bees. O, how in my young days I did dote on the candy pulling and the kissing bee. To my young and unsophisticated mind they were divine institutions; and, even now, after the lapse of so many years when the "heyday in the blood is tame," how I look back upon those few days with unalloyed pleasure.

Among the early pioneers, I mean the great masses, there was a stern code of morals little understood at the present time. Exceptions there were, to be sure, but I refer to the people as a whole. One instance will serve as an illustration. The beaux and belles, in linsey-woolsey and buckskins, were assembled from the country around and about. My father had sent me along with brothers and sisters to bring back the saddle horses, as there was not stable room for all. Other neighbour boys were there on a like errand. We were sitting on our horses and ready to start, when several of the young ladies, among them my sisters, came out of the house and told us to wait. Presently, practically all of the girls came out with hats and riding habits and a consultation was held in the front yard. While they all stood there a man and a woman came out, mounted their horses and rode away. We were then told to go on home with the horses. I afterwards learned that the whole trouble originated in the fact that the lady who had ridden away was a divorced woman. To present-day readers, this may appear absurd, prudish, but not so to the men and women of that day. This is not repeated here to "point a moral," but merely to "adorn a tale" of pioneer days.

For excitement, the frequent Indian uprisings, and more frequent Indian scares, afforded abundant material upon which the young enterprising and adventurous spirits of the day could work off their surplus energies. Hunting, too, afforded a pleasurable and profitable pastime to the young when not engaged in the work of building houses, barns, and fences, and the boy of ten who could not pick off the head of a grouse or pheasant at thirty or forty yards was only fit to be "tied to mama's apron string." In times of danger age was no bar, the boy of 14 marched side by side with the gray haired volunteer, or remained at home to protect "mother and the children." I well remember once when the neighbourhood was thrown into a turmoil of excitement. A large grizzly bear had left his mountain lair and was playing havoc with the cattle and other stock in the valley. News reached the school house and my father at once dismissed school, hurrying to join those in pursuit of the robber. Arriving at home he mounted his horse, and taking his rifle and revolver galloped away to join the neighbours. Now, I wanted to go and see the fight, but was curtly told to stay at home. No sooner, however, than my father had got fairly started than I mounted a pony and followed. I was warned that punishment would follow. But what cared I for punishment at such a time? Go I would, though promised a dozen whippings.

The bear had taken shelter on a small mountain stream that coursed through the valley, and was bordered on either side by a narrow strip of ash, thorn, and rose bushes, while beyond this was the level prairie. In spite of scores of men and dogs the huge beast made progress towards the mountains. Baying dogs and the quick snarl of the rifles marked the rapid progress of the beast which at length reached a wooded ravine near the home of "Squire" Miller, that led up the mountain, where a mile above an old Indian was camped. The bear evidently came upon him unawares, but whether he was asleep or was getting water from the small stream, was never known, for, with one sweep of his mighty paw, the grizzly completely disembowelled the Indian, strewing his entrails fifteen feet on the ground. Half a mile above the body of the Indian the fatal shot, among many, was delivered and the chase was over.

As the neighbours gathered triumphantly around the dead body of the monarch of the Oregon forest I saw for the first time sitting on a horse, a boy destined to make a name in the world of letters, C. H. or "Joaquin" Miller. I remember him as a slender, light haired boy, several years my senior. During subsequent years it was given me to see much of this boy, at school, in the mines and later as an apprentice in the Eugene City Herald, a newspaper of which he was the editor.

CHAPTER 3

The Indian Outbreak of 1855

The years of 1853-4 were years of comparative peace, free from actual Indian wars, and afforded the pioneers an opportunity of improving their farms, building up more comfortable homes and surrounding their families with some comforts and conveniences of civilization. Yet even these years were not free from alarms and stampedes. Time and again swift riders spread the news that the redskins had dug up the tomahawk and had gone on the war path. These scares arose from isolated murders by the Indians, whose cupidity could not withstand the temptations of the white man's property. It was not, therefore, until midsummer of 1855 that hostilities began in earnest. A federation had been formed among all the tribes of Northern California, Southern and Eastern Oregon and Washington. The great leaders of this insurrection were Tyee John and his brother "Limpy," Rogue River Indians, and John was one of the greatest, bravest and most resourceful warriors this continent has produced. Another was Pe-mox-mox, who ruled over the Cayouses and the Columbias, and was killed early in the war while attempting to lead the white troops into ambush.

The outbreak was sudden and fierce, lighting up the frontier with the burning cabins of the settlers. Travellers were waylaid, prospectors murdered and in many instances entire families wiped out, their homes becoming their funeral pyres.

Neither age nor sex was spared. Little children were seized by the heels and their brains dashed out against the corner of the cabin. One entire family perished amid the flames of their burning home. Women were butchered under circumstances of peculiar and diabolical atrocity. A man named Harris, attacked by Indians on the Rogue River, defended himself until killed. His wife then took up the defence of her home and little daughter, and with a heroism that has rendered her name immortal in the annals of Oregon, held the savages at bay until relief came twenty-four hours later.

Mock sentimentalists and fake humanitarians have walled their eyes to heaven in holy horror at the "barbarities" practiced by white men upon the "poor persecuted red man." Yet had they witnessed scenes like those I have so faintly portrayed, they too, would have preached a war of extermination. You and I, reader, have an exceedingly thin veneering of civilization, and in the presence of such scenes of diabolical atrocity would slip it off as a snake sheds his skin. I have seen men as kind and gentle,—as humane—as yourself transformed into almost savages in the presence of such scenes.

For a year previous to the great outbreak, the Indians would leave their reservations in squads, and after murdering and pillaging the settlements, would return with their plunder to the protection of the agencies. Demands made for their surrender by the settlers were answered by a counter demand for their authority, which required delay and generally ended with the escape of the murderers. The result was that squads of Indians off the reservations were attacked and sometimes exterminated. Thus affairs grew from bad to worse until the final great outbreak during the summer of 1855.

Geo. L. Curry, Governor of the Territory of Oregon, at once issued a call to arms and volunteers from every part of the territory instantly responded. A company of U. S. dragoons under command of Capt. A. J. Smith, who subsequently achieved fame in the war of the States, was stationed in

Southern Oregon, and rendered all possible aid, but the slow tactics of the regulars was illy calculated to cope with the savages. The main reliance, therefore, must be placed in the citizen soldiery. Every county in the Territory answered the call to arms, forming one or more companies, the men, as a rule, supplying their own horses, arms, ammunition, and at the beginning of the outbreak, their own blankets and provisions. There was no question about pay. The men simply elected their own officers and without delay moved to the front.

Linn county furnished one company under Capt. Jonathan Keeny and went south to join Col. Ross' command and was joined by many of our neighbours. My two brothers also went with this command, one as teamster, the other shouldering the spare rifle. As previously remarked, age was not considered, the boy of 14 marching side by side with the gray haired man, armed with the rifles they brought from the States. The ammunition consisted of powder, caps and moulded bullets, nor was the "patchen" for the bullet omitted. The powder was carried in a powder horn, the caps in a tin box, the bullets in a shot pouch and patchen for the bullets was cut out the proper size and strung on a stout leather thong attached to and supporting the shot pouch and powder horn.

In the fall after the departure of the first contingent, and at a time when families were practically defenceless, news reached us by a tired rider that 700 Indians had crossed the trail over the Cascade mountains and were burning the homes and butchering the settlers on the Calapooya, twenty miles away. The news reached us in the night, and one can easily imagine the confusion and consternation that everywhere prevailed. To realize our situation one must remember that most of the men and about all of the guns had gone south. I shall never forget the awful suspense and dread that prevailed in our home as the family sat in a group through the long weary hours of that night, anxiously awaiting the return of the day, yet dreading what the day might bring forth. Horses were gathered and securely tied about the house, and such arms as we possessed made ready for instant use. At last day broke, and searching with the eye the almost boundless prairie, no enemy was in sight.

As the sun rose above the rim of the distant mountains my father determined to disprove or verify the rumour. Neighbours sought to dissuade him, but mounting a swift horse he started for Brownsville on the Calapooya. Meantime everything was in readiness for forting up should it become necessary. The day wore on, still no news. In vain we gazed from the house top over the prairie for a sight of a horseman. Doubt and uncertainty as to the fate of my father and our own fate was almost worse than death. The day wore on. Would father never return—had he been killed? were the questions whispered one with another. My mother alone was confident, relying on father's discretion and the further fact that he was riding the swiftest horse in the Territory. At last near sunset we descried him galloping leisurely toward home. When within a short distance he settled into a walk, and we then knew that the danger, at least for the present, was not imminent. The only emotion manifested by my mother was a stray tear that coursed down her pale and trouble-worn cheek. My father reported a false alarm, originating in the overwrought imagination of settlers on the exposed margin of the valley.

At other times the alarm came from the west side of the river. Fears were entertained that the savages from the south would cross over the Calapooya mountains and attack the settlements in Lane county. One settler had a large bass drum, and the beating of this, which could be heard for miles, was the signal of danger. More than once the deep roll of the drum roused the country, only to discover that it was a false alarm. But these constant alarms were trying indeed, especially on the timid and nervous, and women became almost hysterical on the most trivial occasions.

Time wore on, and at length the news came of the defeat of Col. Ross' volunteers and Capt. Smith's dragoons. Many were killed with no compensating advantage to the whites. Among the number killed was one of our neighbour boys, John Gillispie, son of a minister, and my father and mother went over to their home to convey the sad news and to render such poor consolation to the parents as was possible. Every family in the land had one or more of its members with the troops, and any day might bring tidings of death or even worse. Hence there was a close bond of sympathy between all. Happily, the death of young Gillispie was to be the only one to visit our neighbourhood.

The stay-at-homes, those gallant (?) soldiers who fight their battles with their mouths, were loud in fault finding and severe in censure of those in command, and would tell how the battle should have been fought and how not. This was especially true of the one-horse politicians, too cowardly to go to the front, and of disgruntled politicians. To the shame of our common humanity be it said, there were not wanting those who sought to coin the very blood of the brave men at the front, and these ghouls and vampires talked loudest when the war was at length brought to a close, to be quoted in after years as history by Bancroft and others.

Chief John adopted a Fabian policy from the first. He would disappear with his warriors, hiding away in the deep recesses of the mountains only to appear again when and where least expected, but towards the close of 1856 his people grew tired of war. They said the more men they killed the more came and took their places, and in spite of John and Limpy they determined to sue for peace. The terms were finally agreed upon, and John and Limpy, deserted but not conquered, at last surrendered.

After the surrender, John and son, a lad of 16, were placed on board a steamer and started to a reservation up the coast. When off the mouth of Rogue River and beholding the hunting grounds of his people and the familiar scenes of his youth, he made a desperate attempt to capture the ship. It was a "Call of the Wild," and snatching a sabre from his guard he succeeded in driving them below and for a time had possession of the ship's deck. But firearms were brought into play, one leg of the boy was shot off and John, badly wounded, was placed in irons. He told his captors that it was his purpose to capture the ship, run her ashore and escape into the mountains. On a reservation, John spent the remainder of his days,—a captive yet unconquered save by death. As previously stated, in point of courage, cunning, savage ferocity and soldierly ability and generalship, Tyee John has had few equals and no superiors on the North American continent.

It was not my purpose to attempt a detailed history of the Rogue River war as that task were better left to the historian with leisure to delve into the musty records of the past, but I sincerely hope that when the true story of that bloody time is written the kernel of truth will be sifted from the mass of chaff by which it has thus far been obscured. My purpose is merely to give the facts in a general way as I received them, and the conditions surrounding the pioneers of which I was one. The true story of the Rogue River war is but a duplicate of many other Indian wars. It is a story of incompetent, bigoted, self-opinionated, Indian agents, wedded to form and red tape, without any of common sense or "horse sense," required in dealing with conditions such as existed prior to the breaking out of the war.

The early immigrants to the Oregon, and indeed, to the Pacific coast, merely sought to better their conditions. They came with their flocks and herds, their wives and their children, their school books and their Bibles, seeking not to dispossess or rob the occupants of the land. They found a vast empire, of which the natives were utilizing but a small portion. There was room for all and to spare. The natives at first received the white strangers with kindness and hospitality. There were exceptions even to this rule, but it was the exception. The white man's property soon excited the cupidity of the Indian, and knowing no law but the law of might, he sought to possess himself of the same. And right here I want to say, that from an experience covering more than half a century, the only thing an Indian respects on earth, is Power. Courage he respects for the simple reason that courage is power. And I might further add, that this rule applies with equal force to the white as well as to the copper-coloured savage.

Treaties had been made with the Rogue Rivers and the Umpquas but in a true sense were not treaties, but, on the part of the Government, merely bribes to be good. They moved to reservations, enjoyed the blankets and other good things provided by the Government so long as it suited them. Then they would steal out of the reservations, rob, murder and plunder the settlers, and return to the protection of the agents. Tracked to the reservations, the agents refused to surrender them. The red tape here interposed and red handed murderers were saved, that more murders might be committed. Instead of the Government and the agents being a protection to the settlers, they were the protectors of the Indians, and as sometimes happened, troops were called upon to lend a helping hand. Such conditions could not last—such outrages could not be endured. Hence when bands were caught off the reservations they were destroyed like dangerous, noxious beasts.

Apologists of murder and rapine have held up their hands in holy horror at such acts on the part of the settlers. The "poor, persecuted people," according to them, were foully wronged, massacred and exterminated. They saw but one side, and that was the side of the savages. With the close of the Rogue River war, the Indian question west of the Cascade mountains was settled forever. John and Limpy had made a heroic struggle for the hunting grounds of their fathers and incidentally for the goods and chattels, and the scalps of the white invaders. But, moralize as you may, the fiat of God had gone forth; the red man and the white man could not live peaceably together; one or the other must go. And in obedience to the law of the survival of the fittest, it was the red man that must disappear. It was, in my opinion, merely a continuation of the struggle for existence—a struggle as old as man, which began when "first the morning stars sang together," and will continue till the end of time. That law applies to all creatures. Take for instance, the lower order of animals. In the tropics the deer is small, not much larger than a coyote. The weakling as well as the strong and vigorous can survive. Further north, where conditions are harder, the deer is larger. Continuing on north, where only the strong and vigorous can survive the rigors of winter, we find the caribou.

It may be pointed out that the largest animals of earth are found in the tropics, where the struggle for existence is least severe. Yet in the frozen mud of Siberia and Alaska we find the remains of animals the elephant and the mastodon—compared to which old Jumbo was but a baby. And imbedded in the asphalt of Southern California is found the remains of the sabre toothed tiger, by the side of which the royal Bengal is but a tabby cat. But I am getting into deep water, and will leave this question for the naturalist, the geologist and the theorist. And the passing of the "noble red man" to the gentleman in silk gown and slippers—and to the sentimental novelist.

Oregon settlers now had leisure time for building up their homes, so better houses were erected, fields were fenced and ploughed, school houses and churches built, scythes and axes were wielded in place of the rifle that now rested in idleness above the cabin door. A new era had dawned on the Oregon, and gentle peace like a brooding spirit hovered above the erstwhile desolate land.

During the succeeding years, up to 1861, there was little to distract the attention of the pioneers. My time was occupied during that period in assisting on the farm during summer and attending the district school during the winter. The loop holes in the wall of the old school house for the rifles had been boarded up, and the larger boys no longer "toted" their guns, and stacked them in the corner.

On the east side of the Cascade mountains, however, the gentle savage was lord of all the lands over which he roamed. Here he was yet master, and thereby hangs a tale. In 1845 an immigrant train attempted to enter the Oregon by way of the "Meeks cut off." With them were the Durbins, Simmons, Tetherows, Herrins and many others I cannot now recall. The history of that journey is one of hardship, starvation, and death. After enduring sufferings such as sicken one in the bare recital the remnant staggered into the settlements, more dead than alive. They crossed the Cascade mountains, coming down the Middle Fork of the Willamette river, and somewhere west of Harney Valley they stopped on a small stream. An old Indian trail crossed at that point, and the oxen in sliding down the bank to water uncovered a bright piece of metal. It was picked up and taken to camp, where a man who had been in the mines in Georgia pronounced it gold. He flattened it out with a wagon hammer, and was quite positive it was the precious metal. But men, women and children subsisting on grasshoppers and crickets and fighting Indians most of the day, had something else to think about.

The incident, therefore, was soon forgotten amid the dire stress of their surroundings. But when gold was discovered at Sutter's Fort in California, Sol Tetherow called to mind the finding of the piece of metal on the banks of the stream not far from Harney Valley. He told about it—told and retold the story, and as the stories from California grew, so grew the story of the old man, until finally he declared he could have "picked up a blue bucket full in the bed of the creek." Hence originated the name, the "Blue Bucket Diggins."

During the years of 1857-58-59-60 and 61, companies were formed in the valley counties to search for the "Blue Bucket Diggins." The companies were loosely formed, with little or no discipline, and were, therefore, predestined to end in disaster. After crossing the mountains and seeing no sign of Indians, the officers had no power and less inclination to enforce discipline. There being no signs of Indians, it was useless to maintain guards; they could whip all the Indians east of the mountains, and why attempt to put on "military airs?" They were destined to a rude awakening. Some morning about daylight, twenty or thirty red blanketed men, with hideous yells would charge the horse herds, while a hundred or more with equally hideous yells would attack the sleeping men. Then would result a stampede, those who had talked loudest and talked most about cowards, being first to lose their heads. The few cool heads would make a stand, while the savages after getting away with the horses, would beat a retreat, leaving the gold hunters to straggle afoot back across the mountains to the settlements.

These expeditions served to work off the surplus energy of the adventurous and restless, until the news arrived in the spring of 1861 of the discovery of gold in the Nez Perce mountains. The reports, as in most similar cases, were greatly exaggerated, but it served to create a genuine stampede, and while yet a boy of 14, I was drawn into that torrent rushing to the new El Dorado. In justice to the good sound sense and mature judgment of my parents, I am compelled to say that it was not with their consent that I was drawn into this wild whirlpool, but, I argued, was I not a man? Could I not ride and shoot with the best of them? And, perforce, why should I not go to the mines and make my fortune?

I went. But by way of parenthesis, will say to my young readers—Don't.

CHAPTER 4

I Shoot My Indian

I have now arrived at a point where I shall speak more of myself, and the insignificant part I was to play in moulding history and shaping the destinies of Oregon and the Northwest.

Joining a company of neighbours we crossed the Cascade Mountains by way of the Barlow route. All had saddle horses with one pack horse, or mule, to two men. At Grass Valley, between the Deschutes and John Day River we fell in with a large company returning from a search for the "Blue Bucket Diggins." They, had been successful (in saving their horses) and hearing of the Oro Fino strike were bound, like ourselves, for the new El Dorado.

At the crossing of the John Day River we found a ferry boat kept and owned by a couple of thrifty traders, who had set themselves down to make their fortunes quickly and without the aid of the pick and shovel. But their covetousness was their ruin. The sum of $6 was demanded for a horseman and $4 for a pack horse. Our party argued with them, but to no purpose. They would take nothing less. After parleying for some time the traders were asked the price for ferrying over a foot-man and his luggage. Wall Cushman, one of the traders, replied, "one dollar." Then saddles and packs began to come off the backs of horses and mules. Cushman threatened, swore and plead, but all to no purpose. He should receive one dollar for ferrying footmen and no more.

Saddles, packs, provisions, and blankets were piled up at the ferry landing and the most stupendous amount of luggage ever carried by a hobo was then, one after another, piled on the backs of footmen. The footman would stand within a step of the boat and, after his luggage was piled on his back, would make a step on to the boat, and drop his load. Often two and three men would steady him until the step was made. All was fun and laughter except to Cushman and his partner. While this was going on, others had crowded the horses to the river bank and were endeavouring to make them swim the river. But try as they would, the horses upon striking the swift current of the river would swing around and come out on the same side. It was now Cushman's time to laugh. In this extremity a reward of $20 was offered anyone who would swim his horse ahead of the band and guide them over. I quickly volunteered. I wanted the twenty, and I wanted to save my dollar. Some of the older men objected. But I had swum my horse across the Willamette River and the insignificant John Day, not a fourth as wide, had no terrors for me. Mounting my horse, I rode down into the river until almost swimming. Meantime I had divested myself of all clothing save that provided by mother nature, and having loaded my saddle and effects on the back of my partner, fastened my right hand in my horse's mane and gave the word. Sliding off on the lower side I guided my horse with my hand and he took the current of the stream like a steamboat. The other horses to an animal followed, and in a few moments were all safely on the other shore. The crowd cheered heartily and even Wall Cushman could not restrain his feelings, but exclaimed, "My boy, you are a brick."

The $20 was not only given me, but several who had not contributed to the first "pot" gave a half dollar. Altogether I was handsomely paid for my few moment's work, and as the water was not cold, I rather enjoyed the swim.

From there we went to Walla Walla, following the old Nez

Perce trails. At that time there were not a dozen habitations between the Dalles and Walla Walla, where now is a densely settled country and one of the great wheat belts of the continent. A few days after crossing the John Day I made my first horse trade. An old school teacher in the company fell in love with my horse, and not only gave me a better animal, but almost the value of my own to boot. I began then to flatter myself that I was not only a traveller, but a business man as well. But alas! I had many a sad lesson to learn ere I got my "teeth cut."

Arriving at Walla Walla, then a small village, with a Government post half a mile away, we purchased a few supplies and then pushed on to the mines. Going down the Alpowwa I saw apple trees planted by Father Spaulding, of blessed memory, in 1836. The trees were thrifty and some of them very large, and were being cared for by Nez Perce Indians. The good Father Spaulding, with other Presbyterian missionaries, had come among these people bearing the message of peace and good will and they, with the exception of the rebellion of Chief Joseph, had ever after adhered to his gentle teachings. The Nez Perce Indians are the most intelligent and finest looking Indians I have ever seen. They are also a brave, self-reliant race, and Joseph's band bears the distinction of being the only Indians on the continent with the steady courage to charge an equal number of the enemy in the open field.

We crossed Snake River at Lewiston, then a trading village of half a dozen tents. The ferry boat was towed up the river half a mile by a horse and then rowed across with oars pulled by two men. Lewiston is located at the junction of the Snake and Clearwater, but we went by way of Camas Prairie and crossed at Craig's ferry, and two days later landed in Oro Fino city. Hundreds of miners had preceded us, and when we arrived the ground was all taken up. I, therefore, found a job at sluice forking at $75 per month, a boy's wages. Men were receiving $5 per day of ten hours, but for night work $7.50 was paid.

37

I remained with my job but a short time, having found a better one in a store, more suited to my strength and at better wages. I was also agent for Miller & Mossman's express and received a good commission for all the envelopes sold bearing their name. Envelopes were sold at $1 each, and were carried to Walla Walla by pony express. The Miller here referred to was then plain Heinie Miller, express rider, but now known to fame and the world of letters as "Joaquin" Miller.

The little store where I was employed was located about three miles above Oro Fino city on Rhode's Creek, the richest placer diggings in the district. Sunday was a busy day for miners. Clothes had to be washed, picks sharpened, letters written to the "folks at home," and as often happened, "dust" sent to them also. This had to be carefully weighed on gold scales, a receipt given and the dust marked and placed in a buckskin purse. There was no other means of communication with the outside world, and both letters and dust must be sent by Miller & Mossman's express. To the credit of Mr. Miller, be it said, that thieves, robbers and murderers let him severely alone. Not only that, but no one ever lost a dollar entrusted to Heine's care, though murders and robberies were quite frequent, and it was well known that he always carried a large quantity of gold dust; but they simply didn't want the job of taking it away from Heine Miller.

It was one of my duties to take the "express matter," letters and gold dust, to Oro Fino in time for the Walla Walla express Monday morning. As the express started at 6 o'clock I had to get up early, besides it was deemed safest to "hoof down the trail" before daylight. The trail was a mere foot path cut through the bull pines, in the shadow of which imagination more than once pictured a lone robber. But I always carried my revolver in my hand and, though a boy, I was almost as good a shot as Miller—at least I thought so. However, I always arrived on time and without mishap or accident.

After delivering my express matter I had leisure to walk

about town, view the sights and watch the swaying crowds of gamblers, sure thing sharps and other forms of human flotsam and jetsam as they fleeced their victims, the miners. One occasion I shall never forget. It was the funeral of one of the prominent citizens of Oro Fino. The aforesaid prominent citizen bore the euphonious cognomen of "Bob-up-the-creek." Bob, probably at his christening, was given another name answers as well as another, especially among the aristocracy of which Bob was an honoured member. Bob was a bad actor, too, especially when under the influence of liquor. One Sunday Bob imbibed quite freely and finally "declared himself chief." There were none who cared to dispute with Bob his self assumed title, but he finally ran "up against" an old Frenchman who kept a pie stand. Bob concluded to take possession of the stand, but his right to do so was disputed by the Frenchman. To settle the dispute the Frenchman emptied the contents of a double barrelled shot gun into Bob's head. That settled the dispute and likewise Bob.

Being a citizen of prominence, his friends and admirers determined to give Bob a respectable send off. Accordingly a neat coffin was purchased and Bob reverently placed therein. A procession was formed and from fifty to seventy-five of his friends followed his remains to the newly made cemetery on the hill. All were in full dress—black pantaloons, checked flannel shirt with white collar, and with a revolver and knife swung conveniently to the belt. Now, no self-respecting or prudent gentleman of the class of which I am speaking, moved abroad in those days without the ever handy knife and pistol. As the occasion was one of importance, I followed after the procession. Arriving at the grave, the coffin was placed upon two poles laid across the vault. The burial service was then read by one of the mourners, a faro dealer, if my memory serves me right, a solemn hymn was sung and then all that was mortal of "Bob-up-the-creek" was consigned to the grave. Four lusty mourners then began shovelling in the dirt. When the grave was about two-thirds filled, a repulsive looking vagabond, the town drunk, threw himself across the grave bellowing like a bull buffalo, and exclaiming "here is a poor soul gone to eternity and not one tear shed over his grave." Meanwhile the dirt kept falling—it appeared to me a little faster, when the old drunk, seeing himself about to be buried alive, crawled upon his feet, shaking himself very much as a wet dog is wont to shake himself. This action was greeted with peals of laughter and shouts from the mourners. Such was the funeral of "Bob-up-the-creek." Shocked and disgusted I turned and walked down the hill to town, to be followed soon after by a laughing, jesting crowd, who dispersed to their different "places of business" to lie in wait for the unwary sucker, the miner.

I remained at the store until the proprietor, Mr. Vaughn, sold out, and hearing that a company was being formed at Pierce City to go to the Blackfoot country on a prospecting expedition, I went there and applied to the, leader for admission. He looked me over, smiled and said that it was too dangerous an expedition for a boy. I replied that I supposed there was danger, that I was not afraid and could shoot as good as any of them. At this the men listening began laughing and the leader told me he didn't want me. Indignant, I turned away, but was followed a little way by a rather pleasant looking man. He said, "My boy, you are too young to go with the crowd. They are a rough set and not fit for a boy of your age to associate with." He then shook hands with me and bade me good bye.

I returned to Oro Fino, and as winter was approaching, I joined a strong party and started back to Walla Walla. This was deemed prudent, for besides the robbers, there were rumours of Indian troubles after we should have passed beyond the Nez Perce country. About this time we began hearing rumours of the Battle of Bull Run, and this formed the chief subject for conversation around the camp fire of evenings. At Lewiston a very dignified Indian, a Nez Perce, asked permission to join our company to Walla Walla. He was accompanied by a boy about 16 whom we judged to be his son. Permission, of course, we readily granted and we proceeded on our way. That evening the usual subject of conversation came up, Northern and Southern men good naturedly discussing the news, and each construing a victory for his side. Finally the Indian spoke up and said, "I think, gentlemen, I can settle your controversy. I have received the latest papers and all are agreed that the battle resulted in a disaster to the Federal arms." All looked at him in astonishment, but he continued and gave us a vivid description of the battle. We at once knew the speaker to be none other than Lawyer, chief of the Nez Perces, scholar and graduate of an eastern college, and one of the bright men of any race red or white. I met him after our arrival at Walla Walla and recognized in the superbly dressed man our fellow traveller. He wore a broadcloth suit, silk hat and carried a gold headed cane. His son was also well dressed.

Again following the old Nez Perce trails, which everyone who has travelled over that country during the early days will remember, we proceeded to the John Day River. Here I met some old Lane county friends, a Mr. Driskol and his son, a young man of about 21 years of age. They had driven over the mountains a band of cattle and turned them on the range at John Day and Rock Creek. Two brothers named John and Zim Smith, from Douglas county, had also driven out cattle and turned them loose on the same range. The Smiths had returned to the valley, but were expected back in a week or such a matter.

Driskol and his son now asked me to remain with them and assist in rounding up the cattle preparatory to leaving them for the winter. They would pay me good wages and then, the Smiths returning, we would all go home together. The free wild life of the prairie having an almost irresistible charm for me, it did not require much persuasion to induce me to remain.

Our task consisted in riding the river and tributary streams and driving the cattle back on the range. The men at the ferry told us that the Columbias were friendly and to be trusted. They cautioned us that the country further up the river and Rock Creek was frequently raided by roving bands of Snake Indians. These savages were hostile at all times, and this was one reason it was desirable to prevent the cattle straying too far and thus falling an easy prey to the Snakes. They also said it would be prudent to keep a sharp lookout when riding too far south. We continued riding and driving in the cattle for a couple of weeks, hoping for the return of the Smiths before venturing too far. But they not returning, we decided to go up Rock Creek above the cattle and drive them down.

The first day we travelled leisurely along and made about twenty miles. That night we camped and made our beds in a rye grass bottom, having previously cooked our supper and riding until after dark. This was done to prevent any roving band of Snakes that might be in the country from discovering our camp and attacking us at disadvantage. The old gentlemen Driskol was uneasy and he and his son watched our camp time about. I offered to take my turn, but the old gentleman said "the boy will go to sleep," an arrangement very satisfactory to a tired, sleepy-headed boy. The next morning we packed up and rode to a favourable place and cooked our breakfast. While we were eating an Indian rode into camp, who hailed us in jargon and we assumed at once that he was a Columbia. He said he had lost a horse while deer hunting and if we were going any further south he would like to travel with us. We thought little of the matter and readily gave permission, the more so as he carried a good rifle and would be a welcome addition to our party in the event of a "scrap" with the Snakes. As we proceeded up Rock Creek, we still found cattle tracks and were loath to turn back. We halted at noon to rest our horses and cook our dinner by the side of a pool in the bed of a creek. While the younger Driskol was getting dinner, the elder Driskol keeping a watch, a wild goose lit in the pond 20 feet away. Picking up my rifle I shot its head off. I will now confess that if ever a foolish, thoughtless boy got a scolding I got it then and there, from the elder Driskol. He declared I was trying to bring "the Snakes right down to murder us all." I was sorry of course for my thoughtlessness, but all the same I got my goose. That evening that goose was the subject of many lectures, was in fact a continued story.

As evening wore on and we were getting further and further away from our camp on the John Day, we were more than usually careful. Patches of willows, narrow canyons and high rye grass bottoms were avoided. In fact, we kept on open ground where we could see an enemy several hundred yards away. We figured that in an open field fight we could more than hold our own, notwithstanding the fact that we were only four in number, counting the Indian. But by-and-by, our travelling companion became a source of considerable uneasiness. When questioned regarding his lost horse he did not give straight replies, but was evasive and somewhat contradictory, and Mr. Driskol began to have suspicions regarding his friendly intentions. But what to do, or how to rid ourselves of his presence, was a puzzling question. Besides, we felt that we were safer where he could be watched than if out of our sight. That night, after eating our suppers, we travelled some distance after dark and stopped on a level piece of ground away from the creek bottom. We felt safer in the open country than in the high rye grass, especially on account of our Indian companion. We were very careful not to let the Indian see that we were suspicious of him, and after unsaddling and unpacking our horses all but the elder Driskol rolled up in their blankets, the Indian choosing a spot about ten steps away from us. Before lying down, it was deemed best to keep a strict watch on our fellow traveller, and if necessary keep him with us if we had to make him a prisoner. Of course nothing was said to him about keeping watch. During the night he was several times detected, cautiously rising on his elbow and looking around. Discovering the guard he would lie down with a grunt as if with satisfaction.

When daylight came we started to saddle up and load our two pack horses, intending to go some distance upon our return trip, before stopping for breakfast. Saddles were on the riding horses and the Driskols were loading the packs. I had been directed to keep a close watch on the Indian, "and if he attempts to get away, shoot him," said the elder Driskol. They were perhaps twenty steps away, and one of the pack horses starting off, the young man went to bring him back. The old gentleman was busy with the pack, when suddenly, quick almost as a flash, the Indian leaped upon young Driskol's horse and started off. The movement took me by surprise and for an instant I sat as if stupefied. Then seeing the rascal going like sin, I raised my rifle, took deliberate aim, and fired. The Indian threw back his head and throwing his arms aloft, plunged headlong into the grass.

"There goes that d——d boy, shooting another goose," said old gentleman Driskol, almost without looking around.

The young man, however, saw his horse galloping in a circle back to the other horses. Meantime I had dropped my muzzle loader and with revolver stood looking at the Indian kicking in the grass forty rods away. Mr. Driskol now ran up to where I was standing and pointing to the Indian, I said, "It wasn't a goose this time, Mr. Driskol."

We were now all thoroughly alarmed, and imagined the Snakes would be down upon us in no time. Hastily fastening the packs, we then took the lock off the Indian's gun and breaking the stock, threw it away. The pony, belonging to the Indian was unsaddled and turned loose, and we pulled out for the "home camp" in a hurry.

Why the Indian came to our camp we could never understand. He would have stood a better chance of stealing our horses by watching the camp, then slipping in upon us in the night and driving them away, unless it was to throw us off our guard. The probabilities are that he was either a Snake or a renegade Columbia or Umatilla Indian, and counted on getting our horses. Finding we were on our guard, and seeing an opportunity of "swapping horses" while the men were busy, paid no attention and gave no thought to the boy. Certain it was our, or rather the old gentleman Driskol's watchfulness, that saved us from being left afoot forty miles from home. Whether he had confederates, we never knew, as we lost no time in putting as many miles between us and the "Snake country" as possible. During the day we kept in the open country, avoiding any point where an advantage could have been taken of us. We of course talked over the affair of the morning, but not once was the goose mentioned by Mr. Driskol. He did not even refer to the goose when apologizing to me for scoldings he had given me.

We arrived late at night at the ferry, and found everything in turmoil of excitement. Two men, an old man and his son, Briggs by name, if I remember correctly, had been killed by the Indians in Tye Valley, about thirty miles away. The murders created intense excitement, all fearing it was the signal for a general massacre of the settlers around the Dalles and the isolated traders on the Walla Walla road. The Smith brothers had returned and had been assisting the two men at the ferry in fortifying the post. The house, a mere shack, was being walled in with rock, port holes for the rifles being left. Our absence had created uneasiness on the part of the Smiths, but they knew it would be futile to attempt to find us. Besides, it was thought more than probable that we had already been massacred and to undertake to find us would be only to throw their own lives away.

Their surprise and pleasure was therefore great when we rode into the station at 11 o'clock at night. They at once informed us of the murder of the old man and his son, and heartily congratulated us when in return we told them of our own adventure. The two men at the ferry were positive that the Indian did not belong in that section, and by our prudence, they said, we had saved our horses and probably our lives. The next day we all joined in completing the fortifications, and when finished felt that we could "stand off" two or three tribes. Yet, notwithstanding our confidence, we felt that in the event of a general outbreak we were still in a dangerous position and that every care should be exercised. Upon my own part, I felt no uneasiness. Zim Smith was there, a rollicking devil-may-care fellow, and I believed he alone was the match for all of the Indians east of the Cascade Mountains. A careful guard was maintained, however, our horses kept near at hand, and we anxiously awaited results.

Several days thus passed. The Smiths and Driskols seriously discussing the situation. They had ventured their all in the cattle speculation, and to abandon them to the mercy of the red devils was an alternative hard to contemplate. But what could four men and a boy do opposed by hundreds of blood thirsty savages? Under all the circumstances, it was finally determined to embrace the first opportunity of getting out of the country. Our lives, they argued—I had no say—were worth more than cattle. Besides, we could not save the cattle cooped up in a stone fort as we were. We knew that the news would be carried to Walla Walla and that returning miners would travel in strong parties.

A few days later a company of forty or fifty men came along, and as they were well armed, we determined to join them. The two men at the ferry also abandoned the place and went with us.

I omitted to say that Wall Cushman, one of the owners of the ferry, had gone below some time before my arrival there, and I had no opportunity of renewing my acquaintance of the spring before.

We arrived at the Dalles without incident worthy of mention. There I sold my horse, saddle and bridle, rifle and revolver to a man who said he was going on a prospecting expedition, and took a Columbia River steamer to Portland. As horses and arms were in demand, not much trouble was experienced in selling, and most of the company with which I was travelling made similar disposition of their "outfits."

Going down the river, Zim Smith, who was quite a talker, told the story of the goose in my presence and in the presence of a crowd. I was terribly mortified, and informed his brother that "Zim was making fun of me." He laughed and mollified my feelings so far as to say, "Zim is only talking and means nothing by it." "In fact, he thinks you are a great boy." But I had made up my mind that I had seen enough of the wild life of the mines, mountains and plains; I would go home and attend school. No more Indians, miners, and rough men for me. I had seen and experienced enough, and was heartily sick of it all. I had experienced a "Call of the Wild" and was satisfied. And I want to say to my young readers again, whenever you experience a similar call—don't.

The trip home was made mostly on foot, the great flood of the early winter of 1861-2 having washed out bridges and roads, seriously interfering with stage travel. An occasional boat made trips as far as Albany and Corvallis, but we failed to make proper connections. Hence from Oregon City to Albany we travelled on foot, but it was a weary journey in the mud.

Here, if the reader will pardon a digression, I will relate a little anecdote illustrative of the times. We were passing through French Prairie in Marion County. The spot, one of the richest and most beautiful in all Oregon, derived its name from the fact that it was settled principally by Canadian French, employees of the Hudson Bay Company. They were typical frontiersmen, hospitable and generous to a degree. We had asked at several farm houses for accommodations for the night, but there was so much travel that all were full and running over. Our party consisted of six, the Driskols, Smiths, Ben Allen and myself. Trudging through the mud, all were tired and hungry. As we neared the upper edge of French Prairie, Ben Allen remarked that he had an old friend, a Frenchman, and he was satisfied we would be welcomed to his home. He lived nearly a mile off the road, but that was better than walking to Salem, six or seven miles. Accordingly, we turned off to the home of Ben's friend. The old Frenchman received us with open arms. He was simply delighted and gave us the best of everything the house afforded. In fact, the old man fairly danced with delight that "Bin" and his friends had paid him a visit.

Seated in home-made rocking chairs, before an open fire place in which was a roaring fire of oak logs, it was, as Zim Smith expressed it, "solid comfort." Finally supper was announced, and the announcement was never more welcome than to that hungry crowd. Besides ham, vegetables and other accompaniments of a farm house dinner, there was a certain stew with dumplings. This was an especially toothsome dish, and all partook freely and with relish. As we neared the end of the meal our host exclaimed, addressing Mr. Allen:

"Well, Bin, how did you like the cat!"

"Cat, h—l" said Ben.

"Oh, yes Bin, he very fine cat. We fatten him three week."

Somehow, our dinner came to a sudden close. Urged by our host to have more, all politely declined, "Bin" saying it was very good, indeed, but he had eaten heartily and didn't care for more.

The next morning we bade our hospitable host adieu, before breakfast, saying we were anxious to get to Salem as we expected to catch a boat for Albany, Corvallis or possibly Eugene City.

That was the first cat I ever ate and since that time I have eaten bear, wild cat, horse, mule, but as a matter of fact, I never ate a more toothsome dish than the old Frenchman's cat—until I discovered it was cat. Hence I am inclined to the opinion that it is all a matter of education.

I arrived at home after Christmas and during the rest of the winter attended the district school. Had I been told that that little district school was destined to be the last I should ever attend, I possibly should have better applied myself to my studies. I remained on the farm that summer assisting in the general work. In the fall of 1862, Joaquin Miller and Anthony Noltner started the "Herald," a weekly newspaper, at Eugene City. Instead of going to school, as my father wished, I applied for and obtained a position as "devil" in the office. Mr. Noltner was of the opinion that the name was very appropriate in my case. However, I soon gained the confidence and esteem of my employers. As evidence of this, I remained three years, and during the time did not lose three days, that is, if we except the several occasions when for a week or two, the Herald was "excluded from the United States mails for disloyal utterances." Publication would be suspended for a week or so and then come out under another name. The columns would be filled with news and "strictly literary matter" for a short time. Then Mr. Miller would launch out and give expression to his opinion on things in general and certain politicians in particular. After a few weeks something said would incur the displeasure of the postmaster, and we would then have to begin all over under a new name. And do you know, I grieve to admit it now, but those little vacations came so regularly that I began to enjoy them—I could go hunting.

Thus Miller and Noltner struggled along, issuing their publication under three or four different names. There was talk at different times of providing Mr. Miller a residence at Fort Alcatraz, with board and lodging at the expense of the U. S. Government. Now, I may be "telling tales out of school" but there are few left to care, save Mr. Miller and the writer, and I trust that "Heinie" will pardon me in thus living over the stirring times of our youth.

In the spring of 1864, I think it was, Mr. Miller sold his interest in the paper to his partner, Mr. Noltner. After that the office had few charms for me, and more and more my spirits bent to a "Call to the Wild." This feeling became the more pronounced by reason of a little misunderstanding with Major Rinehart who commanded the troops at that time stationed at Eugene City. The circumstances leading up to the "misunderstanding," briefly are that a friend, Henry Mulkey, had been arrested for a political offense by order of Major Rinehart, and it had been determined to send him to Ft. Vancouver and possibly to Alcatraz. I went to Major Rinehart's headquarters and applied for a pass to see Mr. Mulkey. That I played good-goody—lied like a tombstone in order to get the pass, is not necessary here to state, but I got it and arranged an escape with Mulkey. That the arrangement miscarried was due to Mr. Mulkey, and not to the prudence of Major Rinehart or the failure upon my part to carry out the program.

Be that as it may. Mulkey was re-captured, and my own arrest was ordered. A little boy, God bless him, overheard Major Rinehart give the order to Lieutenant Tichnor, and ran and told me. Now, I did not relish the idea of a residence either at Ft. Vancouver or Alcatraz—nor did I know how long it would last. Consequently I leaped upon the best horse I saw standing hitched to the Court House fence and rode out of town, sending the horse and saddle back by a son of "Uncle Jimmie" Howard. That boy is now a Baptist minister and I seriously question if he would now accommodate me so far as to return a "lifted horse."

Under all the circumstances, I concluded to absent myself permanently— at least until Major Rinehart's soldiers should move on. Securing an "outfit" I joined a small company in the mountains, crossing the Cascades by McKinzie Pass.

CHAPTER 5

Taking Revenge on Marauding Snakes

On reaching the east side of the mountains, it became necessary to travel in the night, at least through the open country between the Deschutes and Bridge Creek. The Snake Indians were raiding the country, and encumbered as we were with a small pack train, and with only a small company, we deemed that plan safest. During the day a careful guard was kept out and no fires lit. We thus passed safely through the dangerous country to Bridge Creek. We arrived there in the morning and finding quite a company from the Dalles, concluded to "lay by" a day or two and rest our animals.

About 3 o'clock that evening we saw a horseman coming, and riding as if his life were at stake. Coming up, the horseman proved to be Jim Clark, who informed us that the Indians would be upon us in a few minutes and that they had killed his brother-in-law, George Masterson, a lad of 18 years. Horses were at once rounded up and preparations made for defence. While the horses were being driven in, Clark related the circumstances, which left a doubt in our minds as to the fate of young Masterson. Accordingly, and as quickly as possible, every man that could be spared from camp saddled his horse and started back with Clark, either to save the boy or avenge his death.

The circumstances, as related by Clark, were that he and the boy had left the house, afterwards known as the "Burnt Ranch" for a load of fire wood. The house was located on the John Day River about a mile below the mouth of Bridge Creek. Opposite the house the river makes a sudden bend around the point of a high mountain, where the action of water and erosion of time had washed away the base of the mountain leaving a precipitous cliff, hundreds of feet high. Under this cliff a great amount of drift wood has been deposited, and here Jim Clark went for his fire wood. The high bank of the river next the house, which was 600 yards away, had been cut down so as to give an easy grade for loaded wagons. Clark said for the first time they had left their rifles and other arms at the house, immunity from attack rendering them careless.

While loading the wagon they happened to look towards the house, which was in plain view, and saw it in flames. They could also see the Indians around the house. Now the only means of escape was crossing the river, the way they had come. The mountains rose hundreds of feet perpendicularly at their backs, rendering escape impossible in that direction. Hastily cutting the harness from the horses they mounted, and Clark, who was a cool headed man in danger, and brave as a lion withal, told the boy to follow him. As they plunged into the ford they saw a number of Indians lined upon the opposite bank. But it was the only alternative, and the Indians thinking the two men were charging them, ran back out of sight. As they emerged from the river, which here was a shallow ripple, and started up the cut in the bank, the Indians discovered they were unarmed and attempted to close in on them. However, Clark and the boy had reached the top of the bank, and turning their horses up the river towards the mouth of Bridge Creek, sped for dear life.

As soon as they had passed beyond the reach of the bullets and arrows of the savages, Clark tried to persuade the boy to hold up and save his horse. The boy, however, was thoroughly frightened and drove his horse to the top of his speed. Clark, meanwhile, had looked back and saw the Indians mounting, and now began a race, on one side for life, on the other for scalps. The race was prolonged scarcely two miles when young Masterson's horse began to fail. He was then a quarter of a mile ahead of Clark, who, nursing his horse, kept just beyond reach of the bullets. Gradually the gap between Clark and the boy narrowed, and slowly the Indians began to gain. At last Clark rode up beside the boy whose horse was thoroughly spent. He remained beside him until an Indian, riding a black horse, Clark said, ran up within twenty feet of him. The boy saw him raise his gun, and throwing himself from his horse with the exclamation, "O, Lord," was lost to view in the dust. The Indian was at least fifty yards ahead of the others and did not stop to kill the boy, probably leaving him for those behind. Sure of Clark, he kept on, his black and savage heart leaping with joy in anticipation of torturing him.

After tolling the Indian some little distance and coming to a turn in the road, Clark let his horse out and did not slacken his speed until our camp was reached.

As may be well imagined, we did not spare our horses on the return, Clark having been provided with a fresh animal. But it was six or seven miles back to where Masterson left his horse. When we arrived there the search began. But failing to find the body, the awful possibility began to dawn upon us that he had been captured alive. Clark was wild. Had he found the dead body of the boy, it would have been nothing compared to the thought of his capture alive and death at the stake. A search now began for the trail of the Indians, as they had evidently left before our approach. But while this was going on, some of the men found the boy under a bank, shielded from sight by over-hanging earth and matted roots. When pulled out he was more dead than alive, his long bath in the water rendering him practically helpless.

When sufficiently revived, he told us that when he threw

himself from his horse, he leaped into the brush, and coming to the creek, a small stream, ran down until he saw the overhanging bank. He said several times the Indians in their search for him were within a few feet of him.

After finding of young Masterson, we returned to camp. Clark had lost a great deal of property, besides that which had been consumed in his burned home. He was positive the party did not comprise more than fifteen or twenty warriors. He begged us to help him recover his property, or to at least get revenge. Accordingly Perry Maupin, John Atterbury, myself and three others, whose names I cannot now recall, volunteered for the undertaking, making seven in all.

Getting off at daybreak we struck the trail of the Indians and followed as fast as the nature of the country would permit. In places the trail was very dim, and this occasioned considerable delay, but just about sunset the camp of the savages was located. As night was now upon us, it was deemed best to await until daylight to make the attack. We were satisfied they would remain until morning, probably feasting on some of the stolen stock. They were camped on the west branch of Trout Creek about one mile above the forks. Their position was two hundred yards from the creek at a spring, and surrounded by a few scattering willows and quaking asps. On every side was open ground, with a high, bald mountain on the north side, and presenting a splendid opportunity for attack. The location of the camp also indicated that they felt secure from pursuit. Everything being settled, both as to the manner of approach and point of attack, we withdrew and awaited the coming of morning. Unsaddling our horses and picketing them, a portion lay down in an effort to get some sleep, the others standing guard.

At 3 o'clock we saddled our horses and by taking a circuitous route were enabled to approach the camp from the southwest side, and by following a slight depression in the ground reached a point within 150 yards of where the savages rested in fancied security. To prevent the possibility of arousing them by any accidental noise, we had dismounted some distance back, and carefully led our horses by the head, lest a stumble or neigh might discover us to the enemy. It was yet dark when we reached a spot opposite the camp, and standing at our horses' heads, impatiently awaited the dawn. Streaks of light soon began shooting through the eastern sky, but it seemed an eternity before we could see well enough to shoot. Anyone who has ever experienced waiting under similar circumstances will appreciate our impatience and the slow passage of time.

But daylight came at last, and swinging into our saddles, we formed in line and slowly, cautiously advanced. As our heads rose above the slight elevation that had obscured the camp, our revolvers in hand, we spurred our horses into a run and began yelling like furies. Scarcely had we done so when several Indians sprang up and rushed towards us with hands up and calling at the top of their voices:

"Warm Springs! Warm Springs! Wascos, Wascos!"

They were calling in jargon, and recognizing them as friendly Indians, and not Snakes and therefore enemies, both Jim Clark and Perry Maupin called out, "For God's sake, boys, don't shoot!" We halted among them without firing a shot. They then related to us their story. They were camped at the place hunting when the Snakes came upon them about 1 o'clock the previous evening. A skirmish had taken place, but without serious consequences on either side, when the Snakes made overtures for peace, saying they did not want to fight them, that they were only enemies of the white man. They proposed, in order to settle the terms of peace, that the two chiefs, Polina, or as some give the name, Penina, chief of the Snakes, and Qucapama, chief of the Warm Springs and Wascos, should meet half way alone and unarmed.

All the Warm Springs earnestly opposed the meeting, feeling certain that treachery was meditated. But Queapama believed otherwise, and the two chiefs, in sight of their people, went out to the meeting. Scarcely had Queapama reached the Snake chief when he was treacherously murdered by a concealed assassin. Burning for revenge, the Warm Springs renewed the fight, when the Snakes drew off and were seen no more.

They now volunteered to go with us in pursuit of the Snakes, who, they declared, could not be many hours ahead. The Snakes, they argued, could be easily overtaken as they were practically in their own country and would travel leisurely. We knew the two tribes were traditional enemies and the presence of their dead chief was evidence that their friendship for us could be relied upon. The Warm Springs, however, held the Snakes in great dread and never ventured far into their country. The present camp was on neutral territory, and was the main hunting grounds of the former tribe. Polina was especially dreaded, and was believed by the Warm Springs to be bullet-proof. Many told of having shot him in the middle of the forehead, but that the bullet dropped down without injuring him. But may-be-so the white man had "good medicine" and could kill him. Although with such superstitious dread we did not value the aid of the Warm Springs very highly, yet we knew them to be good trailers and skilful scouts, hence their company was accepted, the more readily as we would soon enter the pine timber of the McKay mountains.

Accordingly, after filling our "*cantinas*" with dried venison from the camp of our allies, we again took the trail. Our horses were fresh and as the Warm Springs were such splendid trailers we made good progress, especially after entering the pine timber. The Indians acted also as scouts, skirting each side of the trail and keeping well in advance. No effort had here been made by the Snakes to cover their tracks, and we followed at a rapid pace. The trail led up the west branch of Trout Creek and in a southerly direction. We had not gone more than four miles when we came to the camp of the night before. Their fires were still burning, showing their utter contempt for the

Warm Springs. We followed up Trout Creek to its head and passed through a low gap on to the head of McKay creek, which flows in a south-westerly direction to its junction with Crooked River. Just after passing the divide one on the scouts dropped back and informed us that the enemy was not far ahead. They said the grass cut by the hoofs of their ponies was as fresh as when growing. It was not thought advisable to overtake them in the timber until they had gone into camp. We therefore sent word ahead to proceed with great caution, and to keep well back from the trail. Proceeding now with the stealthiness of a cat creeping upon a bird, the scouts kept well behind the ridges and only occasionally venturing to peep over a ridge or point into the creek bottom down which the Snakes were travelling.

About 3 o'clock they came back and announced that the Snakes had gone into camp about a mile or such a matter ahead. A council was now held to discuss the advisability of attacking them at once or waiting until morning. The Warm Springs were eager for an immediate attack. The camp was located in the edge of an open glade, presenting a splendid opportunity for a close approach. We naturally looked to Jim Clark as our leader and adviser, he being older and far more experienced than any of our party, unless it was our allies. Clark finally advised an immediate attack. "We are getting into the Snake territory, they might move again tonight and we would be compelled to go further on," and, he declared, "we might bite off more than we can chew." That settled the matter, and our allies were in high glee.

It was arranged that a portion of the Warm Spring should approach from the west, keeping well behind the hill, and at the moment of attack should stampede their horses, while we were to make a detour and approach at the point of timber nearest the camp.

After separating we turned to the left through the thick timber, keeping well behind the ridge until we were about opposite the camp. Here we dismounted and tied our horses in a thicket of firs. Silently, almost as shadows, we moved up the ridge and crossing over the crest began the descent through the woods, the moccasined feet of our dusky allies falling noiselessly upon the pine quills. We almost held our breath, lest the least noise, the accidental breaking of a twig, should startle the enemy. Though this was to be my first real Indian fight, I felt no fear and not so much excitement as when stalking my first buck. As we neared the edge of the wood and were almost prepared for the rush, the Indians on the other side raised the yell. Led on by their eagerness they had come into view of the camp and seeing they were discovered raised the war-whoop and made for the herd. The Snakes sprang to their weapons and started to save their horses. Concealment being now useless we burst out of the wood and opened fire. As we did so the savages turned down the creek and fled toward the nearest shelter. I remember dropping upon my left knee, and taking deliberate aim at a big fellow, fired. At the crack of the rifle he sprang into the air and fell, and I then knew I had made one "good siwash." Springing to my feet I drew my revolver, a Colt's navy, and kept with the crowd in a running fight until the Snakes reached the shelter of the woods. To have followed further would have been madness, notwithstanding they were thoroughly frightened and running, as one of the Warm Springs expressed it, "like *klanacks*" (black-tailed deer).

Jim Clark now called a halt. To follow further would result in some of us getting killed, as the Snakes would then have the advantage. Reloading our rifles we returned to count the result of our victory. We found four dead Indians, including one that had had his leg broken by a rifle ball and had been dispatched by our allies, who now proceeded to scalp the dead according to the usages and traditions of their race. It was a gory spectacle, and when they generously offered to divide the bloody trophies, we politely declined, saying the scalps belonged to them, as they had lost their great chief by the treachery of the dead Indians. The operation of lifting the scalp was a simple one. A knife was run around the head just above the ears and the skin peeled off. That was the first I ever saw, and I had no desire to see the operation repeated. Some of those that escaped must have been wounded, but we had no means of knowing the number of these.

The expedition had been partially successful, but keen regret was felt, not alone by our party, but by our allies, that old Polina had escaped. He was the scourge of the whites in all south-eastern Oregon, and while he lived there could be no such thing as peace. He was reserved, however, for the rifle of Howard Maupin, father of the youth who was with us and was kneeling by my side when I fired at the fleeing savages. But that will be reserved for a future chapter. Besides killing four Indians we had captured a number of ponies and some of the stolen stock belonging to the whites. The ponies we gave to our friends, the Warm Springs, besides a captured gun. After destroying everything of value that we could not carry with us, including some camp effects, we returned to our horses and started back. We parted with our friends at their camp of the night before, who lost no time after their arrival there in packing up and, taking their dead chief with them, making haste to reach the reservation as soon as possible.

After bidding them *adieu*, we travelled on our return until daylight when we stopped, unsaddled our horses and picketed them to graze and rest for a couple of hours. Saddling up again we pushed on to Bridge Creek, where we arrived towards evening. We had been in the saddle now, with slight intermissions, for more than forty-eight hours, and rest and sleep were a most welcome boon. Our horses, too, were nearly spent, and here we remained to rest and recruit.

We remained at Bridge Creek several days, recruiting our horses and resting from the fatigues of our recent severe and trying expedition. In reading my simple narrative some may say we were taking desperate chances in following an enemy, outnumbering us several times, into his own country. That is true in a sense. But we had adopted his own tactics, and depended on a surprise. Had we come out in the open and shown ourselves, we would probably have fared badly in such an unequal contest. Secrecy, therefore, was our only safe course, and that required both skill and caution. We knew the Indians would be off their guard, that they would never dream of pursuit, and when surprised would scatter like a covey of quail. Another object was to come to close quarters as quickly as possible, so as to use our revolvers when the rifles had been emptied. Howard Maupin, an old Indian fighter, and father of the youth who accompanied us, once remarked that in "close quarters an Indian can't hit the side of a barn." I understood this when, years after in the first battle in the lava beds with the Modocs, I asked General Wheaton to signal to Colonel Bernard to cease firing and I would charge with the volunteers. We had them hemmed between two lines, with an intervening space of not more than 150 yards. He refused, saying we had lost too many men and the country would not justify the sacrifice of human life. We had fought them all day, and had suffered severely, and finally retreated under cover of darkness. It cost nearly three hundred men to close the Modoc war, including the life of the gallant General Canby. I believed then—I know now we could have whipped them in twenty minutes with the loss of less than a dozen men.

CHAPTER 6

Death of the Shoshone Chief

After a few days at Bridge Creek we joined a pack train going to Canyon City from The Dalles, and though the road was infested with savages, who mercilessly slaughtered small parties, we arrived at the then flourishing mining camp without mishap or adventure. Canyon City at that time was a typical mining camp. There were congregated every known character, race, profession and creed. Under a rough exterior the lawyer, doctor, minister, the rude western frontiersman and the staid and sober farmer, worked side by side. There was no distinction of dress among that restless, surging, throbbing throng of humanity, drawn thither by the all-absorbing motive—the glittering dust that lay hidden beneath the gravel and sands of the streams and along the ravines. The bond of sympathy, however, among the miners was close, and as warm hearts beat beneath the flannel shirts as ever throbbed in the breast of man.

Here, too, were congregated those human vultures that feed and fatten upon the frailties and follies of their fellow-men. The town proper numbered about six saloons to every legitimate business house. Of evenings the gambling hells were a glare of light, and music, both vocal and instrumental, floated out upon the streets to tempt the miners to enter, while away an hour, and incidentally part with their well-earned dust. Some of these hells had "lady waitresses," poor, faded, blear-eyed creatures, in gaudy finery, and upon whose features was stamped the everlasting brand of God's outlawry. These dens of iniquity were only too frequently the scene of awful tragedies, and the sawdust floors drank up the blood of many a poor unfortunate. If the encounter was between two gamblers the miners paid little attention. But if, as was often the case, some miner, crazed with an overdose of "double-distilled damnation," fell a victim to the revolver or knife of a gambler, there was sure to be "something doing." Among these restless, adventurous men there was a semblance of law, but its administration was too often a mockery and a farce. This, however, only applies to the early days of the camp.

One of the saddest of life's tragedies is associated in my mind with an employee of one of these places. His name was Brown, and he was a musician of some merit. He had with him a young and beautiful wife and infant daughter. He played the violin at night and received $10 for each of the seven nights of the week. He was a man of good morals as far as could be observed, and sober withal. One morning he left the saloon at 2 o'clock, as was his custom. From the moment he passed out of the door he disappeared from the sight of men as effectually as the light of an extinguished candle. He was popular and had not a known enemy in the world. But whether he was murdered and his body concealed, or whether he left the country, remained an unsolved mystery. The latter theory had few or no adherents, as he was tenderly attached to his wife and child. Be that as it may. Soon after the disappearance of the musician, a young physician, who was handsome, accomplished, and talented, made his advent into Canyon City. In due time he became interested in the comely widow, and when sufficient time had elapsed, and no tidings came back of the missing husband and father, legal steps were taken, a divorce secured and the young physician made the widow his wife. As years rolled away and the mines "played out," the Doctor and his wife and little girl moved to a town in the Willamette valley. There he prospered, gaining not only gold but that which is far more precious the love and respect of his fellow-man, and, being a public-spirited man, he took an active interest in political and other public matters. In the campaign of 1874 he received the nomination from his party for State Senator. His election was a foregone conclusion, as his party had not only a majority of votes, but his talents as a speaker and his popularity among all classes were in his favour. About that time, however, the exposures regarding the past life of Senator John H. Mitchell were given to the world by the press of Oregon. To offset the charges, there were dark hints and innuendoes thrown out about the disappearance of Brown and the subsequent marriage of the widow to the young doctor. The talk was easily silenced, as it was shown that the doctor came to Canyon City after Brown's disappearance; but it was enough to sting the proud, sensitive heart of the young man to the quick. The mere fact that a suspicion of dishonour attached to his name was sufficient to cause him to withdraw from public life forever. As an orator he had few equals and no superiors, and only for his innocent connection with the Brown tragedy at Canyon City would have achieved a name the equal of that of his distinguished brother, Senator and Vice-President Hendricks of Indiana.

Dr. Hendricks and his wife have long since passed over the river, to the white walled city of God. And there, let us hope, their rest will be eternal, and that the poison tongue of slander will come not to blast, to blacken and to sting.

I remained at Canyon City and vicinity until September and then returned to the valley. During the summer and fall many depredations were committed by Indians. A party of eight men prospecting in the mountains to the west were surprised and all killed. Everyone had died apparently in his bed. The little stream, a tributary of the south John Day river, was ever after known as "Murderers' Creek." The next year, I think it was, Joaquin Miller, then judge of Grant county, led a company of a hundred miners against the Snakes in Harney valley. He was joined by Lieutenant, now Judge Waymire of Oakland, in command of a troop of U. S. volunteers. They were repulsed with some loss and returned without accomplishing anything of importance. The war dragged along until the summer of 1867, when Chief Polina led a band of warriors into the John Day country north of Bridge Creek, where they robbed a settler named Clarno of a number of cattle and horses and started back. Howard Maupin then lived at Antelope valley, 15 miles from the Clarno place. The Indians attempted to capture his horses in the night, but were frustrated by the watchfulness of the dogs that gave the alarm. The horses were corralled, and Maupin and his son and a young German stood guard all night. The next morning Jim Clark and John Attebury arrived at the station, and it was determined to follow and punish the Indians and recover the stolen stock. They followed the trail into the rough brakes of Trout Creek and located the camp. The Indians had halted in a small basin on the mountain side through which ran a small branch, bordered with willows, where they had killed an ox and were enjoying a feast. The five men approached as near as possible and then leaving their horses made their way up the ravine upon which the unsuspecting savages were camped. Howard Maupin was armed with a Henry rifle, a present to the old hero from General George Crook. Silently the men made their way up the rough and rugged ravine until they lay concealed seventy yards away. Taking deadly aim the five men fired, killing four Indians. The Indians fled to the protection of a rugged cliff of rocks, but Maupin's rifle kept following them with deadly effect. One Indian was picked out as the chief and fell at the crack of the rifle. He raised on his hands and halloed to the others until they reached the shelter of the rocks. It required two more shots to finish him, and thus died Polina, or Penina, the leader of the Snakes and scourge of the white man. The shot from Howard Maupin's repeating rifle closed the Snake, or Shoshone war, and peace reigned until their great uprising under Chief Egan in 1877.

For a year or more, or until the spring of 1868, I followed the hum-drum life of a printer. A call of duty compelled me to lay all else aside to care for an invalid brother, Judge J. M. Thompson. He was dying of chronic dyspepsia. Physicians had given him up. He was a mere shadow, and while we had little hope of recovery, we determined to take him into the mountains. As soon, therefore, as spring opened we made our preparations. Our provisions consisted of unbolted flour and salt. Nothing else was taken—no tea, coffee, or indeed anything else save our bedding, guns and ammunition. We journeyed up the McKinzie fork of the Willamette. Game was everywhere abundant and this and bread baked from our flour constituted our only food. It was going back to nature.

A week or so after we arrived at our camp, my younger brother killed a very large bear that had just come out of his hibernating quarters and was as fat as a corn fed Ohio porker. An old hunter endeavoured to persuade my brother to eat some of the fat bear meat, assuring him it would not make him sick. Now, grease was his special aversion, and to grease the oven with any kind of fat caused him to spit up his food. Finally, to please the old hunter, he ate a small piece of fat bear meat. Very much to his surprise, it did not make him sick. The next meal he ate more, and after that all he wanted. He gained flesh and strength rapidly, and it was but a short time until he could walk a hundred yards without assistance. After that his recovery was rapid and sure.

Now, high up on the McKinzie we were told of a hot spring, and that vast herds of elk and deer came there daily to lick the salt that was precipitated on the rocks by the hot water. We determined to move there. But when we arrived we found a rushing, roaring, turbulent river, 75 yards wide, between us and the hot spring. The deer and elk were there all right, the great antlered monarchs tossing their heads in play, but safe as if miles away. In vain we sought a narrow place where we could fell a tree. We found, however, a spot where the water was smooth, though swift as a mill-race, and we determined to make a canoe. Accordingly we set to work, and after many tedious days labouring with one axe and fire our canoe was completed. I was something of an expert in the management of a canoe and when it had been placed in the river, made a trip across. It was a success, and delighted with our achievement, we began ferrying over our effects. One after another, everything but our clothing and cooking utensils were ferried over, provisions, that is, the flour and salt, rifles, ammunition, bedding, in fact all but the above articles. My younger brother was assisting me with the canoe, and the last trip with the last load was being made. Like the pitcher that goes often to the well, immunity had bred carelessness, with the result that the boat was turned over in the middle of the river, and we only saved our lives by swimming. That night we camped beneath the forest giants. A good fire was lighted, bread made on a piece of cedar bark and meat cooked on a stick and eaten out of our fingers. That was indeed getting back to nature, but a more dire misfortune was to befall me the first night. As before stated, we had pitched our camp beneath the shelter of forest giants. Age after age the quills had been falling, forming a mould several inches thick. Before retiring that night I laid my solitary pair of trousers and drawers on the ground before the fire to dry out by morning. They dried. I awoke in the middle of the night to find that my last garments had been consumed, leaving but the waistband of my trousers. The mould slowly dried, the fire had followed, leaving me about the most forlorn individual that ever was blessed with white hide. Now that was going back to nature with a vengeance. In front rushed a roaring, foaming river, and relief was fifty miles away. But what was I to do, but simply do the best I could with a shirt and the waist-band of my trousers.

The next day we constructed a shelter of cedar bark in the event of rain. And now I am going to repeat a story at the risk of being denounced as a "nature fakir." We had with us a band of dogs, trained for hunting. There were seventeen, all told, and of every breed, but with a mixture of bloodhound to give the "staying qualities." We, or rather I, had borrowed them of settlers living on the river fifty miles below. They would chase a bear or cougar all day, and if treed, would remain and bay around the tree until I came. The second night in camp an immense timber wolf came up close to camp and gave a prolonged howl. The dogs all broke away, but they came back faster than they went out. The wolf followed and caught one of them, a large, full-grown dog, and gave him one bite behind the shoulder. The dog gave one yelp and when we reached the spot, ten feet from our bed, he was dead. To make sure that the dog was bitten but once, the next morning I partly skinned him and found that the ribs were crushed and broken. Now if a timber wolf can kill a dog with one bite on the back, why not a young caribou at one bite on the breast? That question I leave to others to solve.

But to return to my forlorn and altogether ridiculous situation. With needle and thread it would have been an easy matter to manufacture a pair of buckskin pantaloons such as I had worn in years gone by and would have welcomed in my present predicament. But needles, thread, scissors, razor and combs had followed the cooking utensils to the bottom of the river. There was nothing to do but simply to "grin and bear it," and I did so with the best possible grace. On an exploring expedition one day I found a tall tree on the bank of the river at a spot where the channel was contracted between narrow banks. I had no axe and therefore set to work to burn it down, but it was a weary task. Day after day I tended that fire, keeping in the shade to avoid the hot rays of the sun, and after six weeks of waiting had the satisfaction of seeing the tree spanning the river, and affording me a means of reaching clothing. But I could not go to the settlements clothed like the Georgia Major, minus the spurs.

During the period of waiting for the tree to fall, I had made a needle of bone and taking an empty flour sack proceeded to manufacture a pair of legs which, with infinite pains, I stitched to the waistband of my long lost trousers and added wooden pegs to insure stability and strength to the flimsy ravellings. In order to form a fair idea of my appearance, one must imagine a youth with a six weeks' growth of hair and beard, a shirt that had to be taken off once a week to wash, a black band around his waist, to which was stitched and pegged parts of flour sacks. I say, imagine all this and you can form some idea of a youth who, under ordinary circumstances, was rather proud of his good looks. My brothers called me "Robinson Crusoe," and I imagine the resemblance between the unlucky sailor, marooned on an island, and a wretched young fellow marooned in the depths of the Cascade mountains without clothing enough to hide his nakedness, was not an inapt comparison.

However, I was now happy. A tree spanned the river and parts of flour sacks covered my limbs, and I would go to Mr. Allen's place, sixty miles below and get my clothing. Crossing the river, however, I discovered that our horses, left in a prairie, had "skipped out." I knew they would be caught at Mr. Allen's place, and the next day I started out. All the dogs followed. They seemed to have an antipathy for my brothers, and, try as they would, they could not make friends with them. Indeed, I have observed through life that children and dogs have an affinity for me. I started in the morning and made about 35 miles the first day, camping and sleeping beside a fallen tree against which I kindled a big fire. After a breakfast of cold bread and venison roasted on a stick, I started on the final lap of my journey. About a mile from Mr. Allen's home is a spot known to campers as "Rock House," where the mountains crowd the river bank, leaving a space of not more than thirty feet between the almost precipitous bluff and the roaring, foaming river. From an overhanging rock a spring of ice-cold water, rivalling the Hypocrene in purity, bursts forth and plunges into the river. The space had grown up with young maples, and the underbrush being cleaned out, formed an ideal camping place for hunters and berry pickers. I was congratulating myself on not meeting a solitary individual when I reached "Rock House" and found it blocked with wagons and tents. I cast one look at the foaming river and another at the bluff. I had passed through some scenes of danger, but never before had I been half so frightened. It was too late to retreat, the bluff could not be scaled and the river was out of the question. Nerving myself, I determined to go ahead, come what might. In front of one of the wagons stood a lady with whom I was well acquainted. I asked her how I could get through. She replied without recognizing me that I would have to go through camp. As I passed around the wagon I came face to face with Judge Lemley's wife. Her home had been my home for years and next to my mother and sisters I reverenced her above all women of earth. She looked at me. I bowed and she nodded her head and I passed on. No sooner had I passed out of sight than Mrs. McDaniels, the first lady I met, ran to Mrs. Lemley and said:

"Did you see that man?"

"O," replied Mrs. Lemley, "it was only some old lousy hunter."

I had made my escape and no one had recognized me. I was jubilant, happy. But horror of horrors! At a turn of the road I came full on a whole bevy, flock, troop or herd of young girls, and at their head was my "best girl." I here submit and affirm, that had I foreseen this, rivers, mountains, grizzly bears, Indians, all the dangers of the wild would have had no terrors for me at that moment. My dogs closed round me and the girls at sight of that "old man of the woods," that awful apparition, ceased their laughter. With sobered faces they shied around me as I strode past, and when fairly safe broke into a run for camp. I heard them running, and in imagination could see their scared faces. But I was safe—no one had recognized me and I was again happy.

Arriving at Mr. Allen's, I related to him the story of my misfortunes. He trimmed my hair, gave me a shave and after changing my "clothes," I once more assumed the semblance, as Mrs. Allen expressed it, "of a Christian man."

That evening I saddled a horse and rode back to the camp. I began then to see the full humour of the whole affair, but it required an hour to convince them that I was really the strange apparition that passed through camp that morning.

CHAPTER 7

My Pistol Gunfight

I remained at the home of Mr. Allen a few days, making frequent visits, you may be sure, to the camp of my friends. I then returned to our camp at the hot springs. My brother had become quite strong and my other brother then decided to return to the valley. Left alone, we indulged in long rambles in the mountains. Taking a pair of blankets each, and baking up a lot of bread, we would strike out. We never knew where we were going, but wandered wherever fancy led. These tramps often lasted a week or ten days. If our bread gave out we simply went without bread until our return to camp. During one of these trips we ascended one of the Three Sisters, snow mountains standing together and reaching to the realms of the clouds. Like mighty sentinels, white as the driven snow, they constitute one of the grandest sights to be seen on this or any other continent. To the north of these mountains and in a valley formed by the angle of the three mountains, we explored the largest glacier to be found in the United States. In this manner the months wore away until the approach of the fall storms admonished us that our wandering life must come to a close, but we had found that which we sought, perfect health. When we went to the mountains in the spring my brother weighed 84 pounds, and when we reached Eugene City on our return he weighed 165, nearly doubling his weight. I had also gained heavily, in fact, nearly 50 pounds.

I mention this that others seeking that most precious of all blessings, perfect health, may know how and where to find it—by simply going back to nature.

Soon after my return to civilization I embarked in my first newspaper venture. I was employed in the office as compositor and foreman and at the expiration of the first month had to take the "plant, fixtures and good will," for my pay. In fact, I was given the office on a promise to run the paper and keep it alive. I so far succeeded that after a year and a half I sold out, clearing $1200. The paper, the Eugene City Guard, is still in existence.

From there I went to Roseburg and started the *Plaindealer*. In this I had the moral support and hearty good will of General Joseph Lane, as well as other citizens of the county. My success was phenomenal, my subscription list running up to 1200 in two years. But as in all else in this world, success was not attained without gaining the enmity and bitter hatred of my would-be rivals in business. Theirs was an old established paper, conducted by two brothers, Henry and Thomas Gale. They soon saw their business slipping away and sought to regain it by indulging in abuse of the coarsest character. I paid no further attention to their attacks than to occasionally poke fun at them. One Saturday evening I met one of the brothers in the post office. He began an abusive harangue and attempted to draw a pistol. I quickly caught his hand and struck him in the face. Bystanders separated us and he left. I was repeatedly warned that evening to be on my guard, but gave the matter little concern. The next morning, Sunday, June 11, 1871, I went to my office as was my custom, to write my letters and attend to some other matters before going to church. On leaving the office I was joined by a young friend, Mr. Virgil Conn. As we proceeded down the street towards the post office I saw the brothers standing talking on the street. One looked up and saw me, evidently spoke to his brother, and they then started toward me. I saw at once that it was to be a fight and that I must defend myself. Some said I could have avoided a meeting by turning in a different direction. Probably I could, at least for a time, but I had started to the post office and there I intended to go. As we approached the young men, one of them dropped behind, and as I passed the first one he dealt me a blow with a heavy cane. At the same instant the other drew a pistol and fired, the bullet taking effect in my side and passing partly through. Stunned by the blow on my cheek, I reeled and drawing my pistol fired point blank at the breast of the one who had shot me. I was then between the men, and turning on the one with the cane, he threw up his hands, as if to say "I am unarmed." As I again turned he quickly drew his revolver and shot me in the back of the head, and followed it up with another shot which was aimed at the butt of my ear. I felt the muzzle of the revolver pressed against my ear, and throwing up my head the bullet entered my neck and passed up through my mouth and tongue and lodged back of my left eye. As I rushed at him he fired again, the bullet entering the point of my shoulder while another entered my body. That was his last shot.

I was taken to my home in a blanket and few thought that I would live to reach it. I was not, however, done for yet, and the next Thursday was out riding with one of my physicians. The affair created the wildest excitement, a noted surgeon, Dr. Sharples, coming from Eugene City to attend me. Throughout the Eastern States there was various comment by various publications, referring to the affair as "The Oregon Style." I refer to the matter here because of the many distorted and unfair stories that have appeared from time to time. It is in no spirit of *braggadocio*, but simply to give the facts. That I deplored the affair, and deeply, too, I freely confess, but only for the necessity which compelled me to defend my life.

On the following February I received an offer to take charge of the *Salem Mercury*. Leaders of the party, among them three ex-Senators, the Governor of the State and many others prominent in the affairs of Oregon, purchased the paper and plant and tendered me a bill of sale for the same. Ex-Senator Nesmith, ex-Senator Harding, Governor Grover, ex-Governor Whitaker, General Joseph Lane and many others urged me to the step. They argued that I could unite all the factions of the party in support of a party paper at the capital of the State. To a young man scarcely twenty-three this was a tempting and flattering offer. I sold my paper, therefore, at Roseburg and with $4000 in money and good paper, and a bill of sale of an office costing $2500, started to Salem. My success there as a newspaper man was all that could be desired. A large circulation was rapidly built up, and a daily as well as weekly started.

In November of the same year occurred the first outbreak of the Modoc Indians and a score of settlers and a few soldiers had been killed. Governor Grover had ordered out two companies of volunteers under General John E. Ross, a veteran of the Rogue River war, to assist the regular army in quelling the insurrection. The outbreak, only for the butchery of the citizens along the Lost River and Tule Lake, was not regarded as at all serious, as a few weeks would suffice to crush or destroy the savages. But as weeks rolled on and still no surrender, nor even a fight, the Governor became uneasy, since he could not understand the delay. Finally, early in January, Judge Prim arrived from Jackson county and had a conference with the Governor. It was scarcely 9 o'clock in the morning when Mr. Gilfrey, private secretary to the Governor, came to my office with a message that Governor Grover wished to see me at his office at once. When I arrived there I found the Governor, Judge Prim and General John F. Miller in consultation. The Governor explained to me that there were stories of needless waste of time, that the Indians had not been attacked, though there were 450 men within a few miles of their camp, that hints of graft were afloat. Would I go in company with General Miller and when could I start? I replied that I would go and by the eleven o'clock train if General Miller was ready.

Perhaps here is a proper place for a short history of the Modoc Indians; their long series of murders and massacres—a series of appalling crimes that have given to their country the name of "the dark and bloody ground of the Pacific." Of all the aboriginal races of the continent the Modocs stand pre-eminent as the most fierce, remorseless, cunning and treacherous. From the day the white man first set foot upon his soil the Modoc has been a merciless foe with whom there could be no peace. The travellers through his country were forced to battle for their lives from the day his country was entered until the boundary was passed. Trains of immigrants, consisting of men, women and children, worn and weary with the trials and hardships of the plains, were trapped and butchered. The number of these victims mount up into the hundreds and constitute one of the saddest chapters in the annals of American pioneers.

Chapter 8

Depredations of
the Modoc Indians

Voltaire describes his countrymen as "half devil and half monkey," and this description applies with equal force to the Modoc tribe of Indians. In general appearance they are far below the tribes of the northern country. They did not possess the steady courage of the Nez Perces, nor the wild dash of the Sioux, but in cunning, and savage ferocity they were not excelled even by the Apaches. In war they relied mainly on cunning and treachery, and the character of their country was eminently suited for the display of these tactics.

Our first knowledge of the Modocs was when they stole upon the camp of Fremont in 1845 at a spring not far from the present site of the now prosperous and thriving village of Dorris. It was here that Fremont suffered the loss of some of his men, including two Delaware Indians, in a daylight attack, and it was here that he was overtaken by a courier and turned back to assist in the conquest of California. From that day to the day when Ben Wright, with a handful of Yreka miners, broke their war power in the so-called "Ben Wright massacre" the Modocs were ever the cruel, relentless foe of the white man, murdering and pillaging without other pretext and without mercy. It has been estimated, by those best capable of giving an opinion, that from first to last not less than three hundred men, women and children had been relentlessly murdered by their hands, up to the beginning of the last war.

The shores of their beautiful lakes and tributary streams are scattered over with the graves and bleaching bones of their victims. Even among neighbouring tribes they were known and dreaded for their cunning duplicity and savage ferocity. They are yet known among the Klamaths, Pits, and Piutes as a foe to be dreaded in the days of their power, and these people often speak of them in fear, not because they were brave in open field, but because of their skulking and sudden attacks upon unsuspecting foes.

During the early 50s many immigrants, bound for Southern Oregon and Northern California, passed through their country, travelling the road that passed round the north end of Rett, or Tule Lake, and crossed Lost River at the then mouth of that stream on a natural bridge of lava. A short distance from where the road comes down from the hills to the lake is the ever-memorable "Bloody Point." This place has been appropriately named and was the scene of some of the most sickening tragedies that blacken the annals of this or any other country. At this point the rim rock comes down to the edge of the waters of the lake, and receding in the form of a half wheel, again approaches the water at a distance of several hundred yards, forming a complete corral. Secreted among the rocks, the Indians awaited until the hapless immigrants were well within the corral, and then poured a shower of arrows and bullets among them. The victims, all unconscious of danger, taken by surprise, and surrounded on all sides, with but the meagre shelter of their wagons, were at the mercy of their savage foes.

In 1850, an immigrant train was caught in this trap, and of the eighty odd men, women and children, but one escaped to tell the awful tale. On the arrival of the news at Jacksonville, Colonel John E. Ross raised a company of volunteers among the miners and hastened to the scene of butchery. Arriving at Bloody Point, the scene was such as to make even that stern old veteran turn sick. The men had died fighting, and their naked bodies lay where they fell. Those of the women not killed during the fight were reserved for a fate ten thousand times worse. The mutilated remains scattered about the ground were fearfully swollen and distorted and partly devoured by wolves and vultures, little children, innocent and tender babes, torn from their mothers' arms, had been taken by the heels and their brains dashed out against the wagon wheels, killed like so many blind puppies. One young woman had escaped out of the corral but had been pursued and butchered in a most inhuman manner. Her throat was cut from ear to ear, her breasts cut off, and otherwise mutilated. Her body was found a mile and a half from the wrecked and half-burned train, and was discovered by her tracks and those of her pursuers.

Again in 1851 Captain John F. Miller raised a company of volunteers at Jacksonville and went out to meet and escort the immigrant trains through the country of the Modocs. Arriving at Bloody point at daylight one morning and finding a train surrounded, he at once vigorously attacked the savages and drove them away, with the loss of several of their warriors. His timely arrival prevented a repetition of the previous year's horror. The savages were followed into the lava beds, but here he was compelled to give up the pursuit, as further advance into this wilderness was to court disaster. The train had been surrounded several days and a number of its members killed and wounded. An escort was sent with the train beyond Lost River and then returned to guard the pass until all the immigrants should have passed through.

During Captain Miller's stay here his scouts discovered smoke coming out of the *tules* several miles north and west of the peninsula. Tule Lake at that time was a mere *tule* swamp and not the magnificent body of water we see today. Taking a number of canoes captured from the Indians to lead the way, and mounting his men on their horses, the spot was surrounded at daylight and a large number of women and children captured. Notwithstanding many were dressed in bloody garments, they were all well treated. They were held prisoners until the company was ready to leave, when they were turned loose.

Another company of immigrants was murdered on Crooked Creek not far from the ranch of Van Bremer Bros. on the west and south side of Lower Klamath Lake. Who they were, where they came from, how many in the train, will ever remain an impenetrable mystery. Waiting friends "back in the States" have probably waited long for some tidings of them, but tidings, alas, that never came. We only know that the ill-fated train was destroyed, the members murdered and their wagons burned. Scarface Charley told John Fairchilds that when he was a little boy the Indians killed a great many white people at this point. The charred remains of the wagons and mouldering bones of the owners were yet visible when I visited the spot during the Modoc War. Charley said that two white girls were held captives and that one morning while encamped at Hot creek the Indians got into a dispute over the ownership of one of them and to end matters the chief caught her by the hair and cut her throat. Her body, Charley said, was thrown into the rim rock above the Dorris house. Hearing the story in February, 1873, while we were encamped at Van Bremer's ranch, Colonel C. B. Bellinger and I made a search for the body of the ill-fated girl. We found the skull and some bones but nothing more. Enough, however, to verify the story told by Charley. What became of the other Charley did not know, but her fate can better be imagined than described.

CHAPTER 9

The Ben Wright Massacre

This so-called massacre has been the source of endless controversy, and during the progress of the Modoc war afforded Eastern sentimentalists grounds for shedding crocodile tears in profusion. They found in this story ample grounds for justification of the foul butchery of General Canby and the Peace Commission. According to their view, these "poor persecuted people" were merely paying the white man back in his own coin, and a lot more such rot.

According to this story, Ben Wright had proposed a treaty and while the Indians were feasting, all unconscious of intended harm, were set upon and ninety of their warriors murdered in cold blood. Captain Jack's father, they said, was among the victims, and it was to avenge this wrong that Canby and the Peace Commission were murdered under a flag of truce. The story was without other foundation than the bloody battle fought by Ben Wright and his Yreka volunteers with the Modoc tribe during the fall of 1852. I will here give the true story as detailed to me by Frank Riddle, one of Ben Wright's men, and which I believe is absolutely true.

In the fall of 1852 Ben Wright raised a company of thirty-six men around Yreka and went out to guard the immigrants through the country of the Modocs. The company arrived in time and safely escorted all trains past the danger point. The lesson taught the year before by Captain Miller had instilled into the savage heart a wholesome fear of the white man's rifle and revolver. They dared not attack the ever-watchful white men openly, but determined to effect by strategy what they dared not attempt in the open field. Accordingly they sent a messenger to Wright proposing a treaty. The messenger, among other things, told Wright that they held two captive white girls, which they wished to surrender as an evidence of good faith. Ben Wright was anxious to rescue the girls and readily consented to a treaty, and promised to kill a beef and have a feast. The Indians in considerable numbers came to the camp, headed by the chief. Wright was then camped on the peninsula, a place admirably adapted to guard against surprise. A feast was had and all went well. The white girls were to be surrendered three days later at the mouth of Lost River, to which place the white men moved, followed by the Indians. The latter were very friendly and exerted themselves to win the confidence of the white men. Three days passed but no white girls showed up. The chief assured Wright that they were coming, that they were a long way off and would be on hand two days later. In the meantime the watchful white men observed that the numbers of the Indians had more than doubled and more and more were coming with each succeeding day. They became suspicious and their suspicions ripened into a certainty that treachery was meditated. At the expiration of the two days Ben Wright informed his men of his plans. He was satisfied that the girls would never be surrendered, but that the Indians, now outnumbering them five to one, intended a massacre. Accordingly he told his men to quietly make ready; that he was going to the chief and if he refused to surrender the girls he would kill him then and there. He warned his men to pay no attention to him, that he would make his way out as best he could; that they must open fire at the instant his pistol rang out; that they were in a desperate situation and must resort to desperate measures or all would be butchered then and there.

The morning was cool, Riddle said, and Ben Wright covered himself with a blanket, his head passing through a hole in the middle, as was the custom of the time, the blanket answering the place of an overcoat. Underneath the blanket he carried a revolver in each hand. He went directly to the chief and demanded that he make his promises good. The chief told him plainly, insolently, that he would not do so, and never intended to do so; that he had men enough to kill the white men and that they were now in his power. But the wily old chief little dreamed of the desperate valour of the man before him, for no sooner had the chief's defy passed his lips than Ben Wright shot him dead. Then firing right and left as he ran, he made his escape out of the Indian camp. Meanwhile, as the first shot rang out from Wright's pistol his men opened a deadly fire with their rifles. For an instant, Riddle said, the savages formed a line and sent a shower of arrows over their heads, but they aimed too high and only one or two were slightly wounded. Dropping their rifles, Wright's men charged, revolvers in hand. This was too much for savage valour and what were left fled in terror. It was now no longer a battle. The savages were searched out from among the sage brush and shot like rabbits. Long poles were taken from the *wickiups* and those taking refuge in the river were poked out and shot as they struggled in the water. To avoid the bullets the Indians would dive and swim beneath the water, but watching the bubbles rise as they swam, the men shot them when they came up for air.

This is the true story of the "Ben Wright Massacre." It was a massacre all right, but did not terminate as the Indians intended. Riddle told me that about ninety Indians were killed in this fight. It broke the war power of the Modoc Indians as a tribe for all time, and from that day the white man could pass unvexed through the country of the Modocs. There were probably isolated cases of murder, but nothing approaching war ever again existed in the minds of the Modocs.

CHAPTER 10

Treaty With the Modocs is Made

On the 14th day of October, 1864, the Modocs entered into a treaty with the Federal government by which they ceded all rights to the Lost River and Tule Lake country for a consideration of $320,000. In addition to this they were to receive a body of land on the Klamath reservation of 768,000 acres, or a little more than 420 acres for each man, woman and child. Immediately after the ratification of the treaty all the Modoc Indians moved to the lands allotted to them, where the tribe remained, and yet remains. This may be news to most of my readers, but it is a fact that the Modoc Indians as a tribe continued to keep faith with the government. The band under Captain Jack were merely renegades who, dissatisfied with their new home, left the reservation and went back to Lost River and Tule Lake. Jack himself was wanted for murder, and sought an asylum in the lava beds, or the country adjacent thereto, where he gathered around him renegades from other tribes—renegades outlawed by Indians and whites alike. Some of the Indians in Jack's band were from the Columbia river region, others from coast tribes, and all were outlaws. One of the leaders, Bogus Charley, was an Umpqua Indian and was raised by a white man named Bill Phips. He spoke good English and asked me about many of the old timers.

In securing his ascendancy over this band of outlaws Jack was assisted by his sister, "Queen Mary," so-called, who lived

many years with a white man near Yreka. In the opinion of
Captain I. D. Applegate. Mary was the brains of the murder-
ous crew who gathered in the "hole in the wall," under her
brother. She was the go-between for the Indians with the
whites about Yreka, where they did their trading and where
they supplied themselves with arms and ammunition, and it
was through her that Judge Steele, a lawyer of Yreka, was in-
terested in getting a reservation for them. Steele made a trip to
Washington to plead their cause, and received a fee of $1000.
He failed, but held out hope to his clients and urged them
under no circumstances to go back to their lands at Klamath,
advising them as counsel to take up lands in severalty under
the pre-emption laws of the United States. It is charitable to
suppose that Judge Steele did not foresee the disastrous consequences of his counsel, yet he knew that Jack was wanted
at the Klamath agency for murder. In furtherance of his advice he wrote the following self-explanatory letter to Henry
Miller, afterwards murdered in a most barbarous manner by
the very men whom he had befriended:

Yreka
Sept. 19, 1872
Mr. Henry F. Miller
Dear Sir. You will have to give me a description of the
lands the Indians want. If it has been surveyed, give me the
township, range, section and quarter-section. If not, give
me a rude plat of it by representing the line of the lake and
the line of the river, so that I can describe it ... Mr. Warm-
mer, the County Surveyor, will not go out there, so I will
have to send to Sacramento to get one appointed. Send an
answer by an Indian, so that I can make out their papers
soon. I did not have them pay taxes yet, as I did not know
whether the land is surveyed and open for pre-emption.
Respectfully yours
E. Steele

Other letters were written by Judge Steele to the Indians. One which was taken to Mrs. Body to read for them advised them not to go to Klamath, but to "remain on their Yreka farm," as he termed the Tule Lake and Lost River country, and told them they had as good a right to the lands as anyone. He further told them to go to the settlers and compel them to give them written certificates of good character to show to the agents of the government, which they did, the settlers fearing to refuse. Shortly after this, Mr. T. B. Odeneal, Superintendent of Indian Affairs, attempted to have a conference with Jack, who flatly refused, saying he was tired of talking; he wanted no white man to tell him what to do; that his friends and counsellors at Yreka had told them to stay where they were.

Under these circumstances the settlers became alarmed and made the Superintendent promise that they should be notified before any attempt to use force was made. How that promise was carried out will appear later on. Early in November, after repeated attempts to induce the Indians under Jack to go peaceably back to the reservation, Superintendent Odeneal determined to turn the matter over to the military. The Commissioner of Indian Affairs directed him to put the Indians back, peaceably if he could, by force if he must. He then referred the whole matter to Major Jackson, then in command at Fort Klamath, who had at his disposal thirty-six men of Company B, First cavalry, and proceeded with his command to Linkville, where he was met by Captain I. D. Applegate, at that time connected with the Indian department and stationed at the Yainax reservation. Captain Jackson was warned by Applegate of the desperate character of the Indians, but informed him the force was sufficient in his opinion if proper precautions were taken. In the meantime Mr. Odeneal had sent his messenger, O. A. Brown, to notify the settlers. Instead he proceeded to the Bybee ranch, carefully concealing from all the proposed movements of the troops under Jackson. Afterwards when reproached by Mrs. Schira, whose husband, father and brothers had been murdered, he gave the heartless answer that he "was not paid to run after the settlers." After realizing the full extent of his conduct—conduct that could not be defended any other way—Brown attempted to cast the odium upon his superior, Mr. Odeneal. However, the latter had a copy of his letter of instructions, hence Brown lapsed into sullen silence.

Major Jackson started for the Indian encampment on Lost River on the 28th of November, leaving Linkville, now Klamath Falls, after dark. He was accompanied by Captain Applegate, and he had supplied his men with twenty rounds of ammunition. Before reaching the encampment he halted his men, saddle girths were tightened, overcoats tied behind saddles and carbines loaded. It was then nearly daylight and proceeding with caution he reached the encampment just at daylight. It was understood that the command was to be divided so as to strike the camp on two sides, thus commanding the river bank and the brush back of the camp at one and the same time. Instead of this, Captain Jackson galloped his troop in between the river and the camp and dismounted, his men forming a line with horses in the rear.

While all this was going on another force, consisting of a dozen settlers, had come down from the Bybee ranch to capture the Hot Creek band on the opposite side of the river from Jack's camp. O. A. Brown had arrived there in the evening but said nothing to any one until 2 o'clock in the morning, when he roused them up and told them that the soldiers would attack the Indians at daylight. They arrived just as Jackson lined his men up on the opposite side. Jud Small, a stock man, was riding a young horse and at the crack of the first gun his horse began bucking. Everything was confusion, the men retreating to a small cabin a hundred yards away, except Small, who was holding on to his horse for dear life all this time. Over *wickiups*, squaws, bucks and children the frightened beast leaped. Just how he got out safe among his companions Small never knew, but he escaped, only to be desperately wounded in the first fight in the lava beds, and later finding a watery grave in Klamath River while sailing a pleasure boat.

After dismounting his men, Major Jackson requested Captain Applegate to go forward among the Indians and tell them they must surrender and go back to the reservation. But scarcely had Captain Applegate reached the centre of the village, when he saw the women running and throwing themselves face downward in a low place between the two lines. He at once called to Lieutenant Boutelle to "look out, they are going to fire." Scarcely had the words escaped his lips when the Indians, concealed under their *wickiups*, opened a galling fire on the line of troops. Applegate made his way back to the line as best he could and as he reached the line he picked up a carbine that had fallen from the hand of a wounded soldier. The poor fellow had just strength enough to unbuckle his belt and hand it to Captain Applegate, who now called to Lieutenant Boutelle that "if we don't drive them out of their camp they will kill us all." Boutelle then ordered a charge, and drove the Indians out of their camp, through the brush and out into the open hills beyond. But this was accomplished by the loss of several men killed and wounded. One Indian had been killed, a Columbia, one of the most desperate of the renegade band. When Applegate got back to where Jackson was standing he had all the women and children gathered around him and while several men had been killed or wounded, he deemed the trouble at an end.

While the above events were transpiring, Dave Hill, a Klamath Indian, swam the river and drove in all the Modocs' horses. With the women, children and horses in their possession all that remained for Captain Jackson to do to insure the surrender of the men, was to take them to the reservation and hold them. What was the surprise of Captain Applegate, therefore, when Jackson announced his intention of turning them all loose. In vain he and Dave Hill protested, but to no purpose.

87

Jackson declared he was short of ammunition; besides, must care for his wounded men. He then told the squaws to pack up their horses and go to the men and tell them to come to the reservation. No more mad, idiotic piece of folly was ever perpetrated by a man than this move of Captain Jackson.

While they were talking two travellers were seen riding along the road some hundreds of yards away. In vain the men on both sides of the river attempted to warn them of danger. The Indians were seen to ride up to them and deliberately shoot them down. This of itself should have warned Jackson of the desperate character of the outlaws. But no, he was either too cowardly to act intelligently or too indifferent of the consequences to act as he was advised. In fact, there is a certain class of army officers who deem it a disgrace to accept advice from a civilian. At any rate he crossed his wounded men over the river in canoes to the cabin held by the party of stock men, and mounting his men went six miles up the river to the ford and put the river between himself and command and danger.

As soon as the squaws and children reached the men, a party headed by "Black Jim" mounted and started down the shores of the lake butchering the settlers. They came first to the Body ranch, where the men were getting wood from the hills and heartlessly butchered them in cold blood. The manner is best told in Mrs. Body's own words in a letter to me in which she says:

"I reside three miles from the Indian camp on Lost River. The Indians had told us time and again that if the soldiers came to put them on the reservation they would kill every white settler. Through hearing of these threats, we requested the messengers never to come with soldiers without first giving the settlers warning. This they failed to do. . . . The male portion of my family, not being aware of any disturbance, were out procuring firewood, and were suddenly attacked within a mile and a half of the house and butchered in cold blood.

About a quarter to twelve my daughter saw her husband's team approaching the house at a rapid gait, and as the team reached the house she noticed that the wagon was covered with blood. Thinking the team had run away she ran up the road to find him. About a quarter of a mile from the house she discovered him. I hastened after her with water, and as I arrived at the spot my daughter was stooping over the body of her husband. Six Indians then dashed out of the brush on horseback. Two of them rode up to me and asked if there were any white men at the house. Not dreaming that there was anything wrong with the Indians, I told them that the team had run away and killed a white man. They then gave a war-whoop and rode off towards the house. On examining my son-in-law, we found that he had been shot through the head.

We then knew that the redskins were on the warpath, and determined to find the other men. Going a short distance we found my eldest son killed and stripped naked. The four horses were gone. About a quarter of a mile further on we saw more Indians in the timber where my husband was chopping wood, so we concluded we had better not go any further in that direction, and made our way to the hills. My youngest son, a boy of thirteen years of age, was herding sheep about a mile from the house when he was killed. They shot him and then cut his throat.

We continued to travel until it became too dark to discern our way, and then sat down at the foot of a tree and stayed until daylight. We then started again, not knowing where we were going, but hoping to strike some house. There was two feet of snow on the ground and our progress was slow and tedious. Finally we arrived at Lost River bridge about 2 o'clock Saturday afternoon. Here we learned for the first time that there had been a fight between the soldiers and Indians. If the settlers had been warned in time not one white person would have been killed, as we all had arms and ammunition sufficient to defend themselves successfully."

The Brotherton Family was not killed until the next day. They lived eight miles south of the Bodys, and like the latter were attending to their duties about the ranch. A twelve-year-old boy, Charley Brotherton, while the Indians were killing the hired man, cut one of the horses loose from the wagon and escaped to the house, where he built a pen of sacks of flour in the centre of the floor to protect his mother and the little children and with a rifle held the savages at bay for three days, or until relieved by volunteers. The house, a two-story box affair, was literally riddled with bullets and how the boy escaped being shot is a mystery. The other settlers, seventeen in all, were similarly murdered. Henry Miller, who had befriended the Indians, was murdered under conditions of peculiar atrocity, for the reason, it was supposed, that he had failed to notify the Indians of the movements of the soldiers as he had promised.

During all these three days of murder and horror, Captain Jackson made no attempt to protect the settlers, but remained forted up at the cabin on Lost River. As soon as the news reached Linkville, now Klamath Falls, Captain O. C. Applegate organized a company of settlers and friendly Indians to protect what was left of the settlement. Captain Ivan D. Applegate also exerted himself in saving the settlers, and did brave work, but there were women and children to protect and days elapsed before an effective force could be gathered to meet the Indians. Meantime news had reached Jackson county and Captain Kelley hastily organized a force of a hundred men and by riding night and day reached the scene of the massacre. It was his company that relieved the besieged Brothertons, defended by the brave boy.

In the meantime the Indians had retreated to the lava beds and bade defiance to the soldiers. General Wheaton, commanding the district of the Lakes, ordered the concentration of troops from Camps Warner and Bidwell, while General Canby sent the forces under Colonel John Green and Major

Mason from Ft. Vancouver to join the command under General Wheaton. As soon as the settlers could fort up for mutual protection, the entire forces of regulars and volunteers were concentrated at Van Bremer's ranch west of the lava beds under General Wheaton and at Land's ranch on the east side of Tule Lake and directly north of the stronghold. Such was the disposition of the forces when I arrived at headquarters at Van Bremer's ranch. By orders of Governor Grover of Oregon the volunteers under Captains O. C. Applegate and Kelley were placed under the command of General Wheaton. The two companies numbered about 225 men, and were commanded by General John E. Ross, a veteran Indian fighter, but too old to withstand the hardships of a winter campaign against Indians. The men were all poorly provided with clothing and bedding, most all having taken only what they could strap behind their saddles, but in spite of this and a temperature often below zero, no murmur was heard, and all anxiously, eagerly looked forward to a meeting with the brutal savage murderers of their fellow citizens. Such were the conditions when I arrived at headquarters.

CHAPTER 11

Battle in the Lava Beds

On Sunday, January 12, 1873, a strong reconnoitring force was sent out under Colonel Perry of the regulars and Captain O. C. Applegate of the volunteers. On the bluff overlooking the lava beds they found the Indians and found them full of fight. A picket was surprised and a gun captured, but they were unable to say whether any of them had been wounded in the skirmish. The Indians, however, came out in force and a brisk skirmish was kept up for some time when the troops, having accomplished the object of their mission, retired.

All the reinforcements having now arrived it was determined to attack the savages on the following Friday. The plans of General Wheaton were submitted to the volunteer officers and fully approved. General Frank Wheaton was an officer of experience and unquestioned ability. He was a veteran of the Civil war, and commanded 20,000 troops at the battle of the Wilderness, besides having the confidence and esteem of officers and men. Every contingency was guarded against, at least as far as it was possible to foresee it. The troops organized for the attack were Bernard's and Perry's troops of cavalry, and Green's and Mason's infantry, numbering 250 men; Captain Applegate's and Captain Kelley's volunteers, numbering 225 men, Donald McKay's Indian scouts numbering fifty and the California volunteers under John Fairchilds and Presley Dorris.

By general field order, Bernard was to move down from Land's ranch on Wednesday, January 16th, and occupy a position not less than two miles from the stronghold. At the same time Colonel Perry was to push across the trail to the bluff with his dismounted troop, while General Wheaton with the infantry and volunteers, ambulances, three howitzers, reserve ammunition, etc., was to go around by Little Klamath Lake and join the command of Colonel Perry under cover of darkness. This was regarded advisable as it was feared that the Indians, discovering our numbers, would leave the lava beds and scatter. Every soldier and volunteer had been ordered to prepare four days' rations, cooked. There was no question in our minds as to whipping the Indians, but we wanted to surround and capture them.

On the morning of the 16th all was astir and as day began to break the troops were all drawn up in line. I had determined to cross the trail with Perry and was sitting on my horse when I heard a man hallo "O," and as I turned my head heard the report of his gun. The fellow, a recruit in Mason's battalion of regulars, had deliberately shot off his great toe to keep from going into the fight. He pulled the trigger of his gun and halloed, before the gun was discharged. I mention this to show the difference in men. Here was a poor weak devil who would rather maim himself for life than to face danger where he might be killed, but it is safe to say that nine-tenths of the rest would have gone on even after the loss of the toe.

We arrived in sight of the rim of the bluff about 2 o'clock and saw the Indian pickets. Colonel Perry threw out a skirmish line and the advance was ordered. Before getting within rifle range the pickets disappeared and we took possession. I now got my first view of the lava beds, as they stretched black and forbidding nearly a thousand feet below. A fog rested over the lake, but we could soon see through the rifts along the lake shore the Indians on horseback coming out to attack us. They appeared like phantom horsemen, and our Indian guide told us they were coming out to attack us, as there were "only a few and they are afoot." A few had reached the bluff and had begun a scattering fire, when we heard several shots that appeared to come directly from the stronghold. The Indian guide told us he thought they were killing some Indians that did not want to fight. As he had relatives among them the poor fellow showed the distress he felt. A few minutes later we heard several more shots, and I told Colonel Perry I heard Bernard's bugle. A few minutes later the clear notes of the bugle rang out clear and distinct, though it was fully five miles away. Yet in that clear, cold, dry atmosphere every note sounded as clear and distinct as though but a mile away. Bernard's column had followed the lake, and under cover of the fog enveloping the shore, had approached much nearer than his orders contemplated. He was at once savagely attacked and all evening the rattle of the guns sounded like many bunches of fire crackers. Repeatedly we heard him sound the charge and we all fretted that we could not descend and join in the battle. Perry's men were desperately afraid that "the Apache boys," as Bernard's men were called, would clean out the Indians and leave them nothing to do on the morrow. But our orders forbade and we contented ourselves with listening to the fight from a distance without being able to take a hand. Toward night the fog cleared away and we had an unobstructed view of the stronghold.

I have often been asked to describe the lava beds. That is beyond the power of language. In a letter to the Army and Navy journal, written at the suggestion of General Wheaton, I compared the Indians in the lava beds to "ants in a sponge." In the language of another it is a "black ocean tumbled into a thousand fantastic shapes, a wild chaos of ruin, desolation, barrenness—a wilderness of billowy upheavals, of furious whirlpools, of miniature mountains rent asunder, of gnarled and knotted, wrinkled and twisted masses of blackness, and all these weird shapes, all this turbulent panorama, all this far-stretching waste of blackness, with its thrilling suggestiveness of life, of action, of boiling, surging, furious motion was petrified—all stricken dead and cold in the instant of its maddest rioting fettered, paralyzed and left to glower at heaven in impotent rage for evermore."

Towards night the rattle of the guns gradually died away and the yell of the savages was hushed for the day. Leaving a strong guard on the bluff we joined General Wheaton a few hundred yards in the rear, anxiously awaited the coming of another day, little dreaming what that day was to bring forth. There was little sleep that night. The frozen ground with a pair of blankets is not a bed of roses, and is little conducive to sleep and rest. Most of the night was spent around the fires until 2 o'clock when all were ordered to "fall in." The order of march and battle was as follows: The command of Fairchilds and Dorris occupied the extreme left along the lake shore; Mason's infantry battalion, with mountain howitzers packed, joined Fairchild's right; Captain Kelley's command occupied the centre with his left resting on Mason's right; Captain Applegate connected with Kelley's right and Perry's left, who occupied the extreme left wing; while Donald McKay's Indians formed a skirmish line in advance. The whole line stretched out a mile or more. As the line filed out of camp, their arms glittering in the bright moonlight, they formed a beautiful and inspiring sight. The command, "Forward on the line" was now given and we moved forward at a brisk walk. I galloped down the line and watched it as it descended the steep bluff. Low down and stretching over the lava beds lay a dense fog, and as the head of the line disappeared it looked as if it were going into the sea. As I sat there General Wheaton came up and insisted that I should leave my horse. On my consenting reluctantly, he detailed a soldier who took the animal back to camp.

As we reached the bottom of the bluff the entire line was deployed in the form of a half wheel, the intention being to surround the savages by connecting with Bernard's left and capture the entire band. Daylight now began to peep through the fog and night, and "forward on the line" was given and taken up by subalterns and repeated until it died away in the distance. There were no skirmishers now. McKay and his Indians fell back and remained in the rear for the rest of the day. Slowly the line moved forward, stumbling along over rocks, but keeping in perfect order of battle. Soon several shots were heard on the extreme right. It was daylight, and someone called that the Indians were escaping around Perry's right. Up to this time I had been with General Wheaton in the rear, but ran out to the line in time to see the Indians in our front leaping from rock to rock about five hundred yards away. The fog had lifted and a clear day was promised. I jumped upon a lava wave and waited for them to stop to get a shot. Instantly a bullet sang over my head, but thinking they were shooting at me from that distance paid no attention, but continued watching the leaping red devils. In about the time that is required to throw in a cartridge and take aim, another bullet went by, but it hissed this time and raised the hair on one side of my head. Still thinking that they were shooting at me from a long distance, I dropped on my knee with rifle to shoulder. Instantly the red devil, with sage brush tied round his head raised up about ninety yards from me and again fired. I only caught a glimpse of him as he made a few zigzag leaps among the rocks and disappeared. I fired at random but failed to wing my game. That taught a rash, presumptuous young fool a lesson, and he contented himself for the balance of the day imitating the men in the line, and keeping well under cover.

"Forward on the line" was ever the command and by 12 o'clock we had driven the Indians through the rocks several miles. Presently word came down the line that the volunteers could not be found. I started up the line when General Wheaton called to me to come back. Returning he directed me to give that order to Donald McKay. It was fortunate for me that I was called back, otherwise I should have gone in behind the "juniper fort," a strong fort built around a stunted juniper tree, and standing on a high point of lava. I gave the order to McKay who was riding a small pony, and he had proceeded but a short distance when the Indians opened on him from the fort and killed his pony. Someone remarked that "the volunteers are firing on McKay," as the shooting was considerably in the rear and to the right. We all ran up on a point when half a dozen bullets came singing around us. For once in my life I was glad as I distinctly saw Col. John Green dodge. He was an old soldier and had probably been in more battles than any man in the army and to see him dodge from bullets was salve to my pride.

A few minutes later we heard a yell to the right and rear as Kelley's and Applegate's men found the fort and charged it on the run. It transpired that it was Mason's line that had given way and the volunteers, feeling their way, had found the fort and taken it. But they lost two men, Frank Trimble and a man named Brown of Kelley's command. Lieutenant Evan Ream of Kelley's company, was also wounded, but he, refused to leave the line after his knee had been bandaged. A large calibre bullet had hit a rock and glancing had struck him on the knee with the flat side, cutting through his clothing and burying itself in the flesh. He was knocked down and we all thought for a time he was killed. He is now a merchant-banker at Klamath Falls. To give the reader a slight idea of the difficulties under which we laboured, I will relate one incident occurring near where I was standing. A soldier was crawling up an upheaval, pushing his rifle before him, when he was shot through the body from underneath.

At about 2 o'clock Col. Perry came down the line and told Gen. Wheaton that he could go no further. A deep chasm, he said, in his front could not be crossed.

"By gad," replied the General, "Col. Perry, you must cross it."

"I can cross it, General, but it will cost me half my command.

Every man attempting to cross it has been killed, and two litter bearers going to the relief of a wounded man were killed."

Word now reached us from Fairchilds that Bernard was calling for help. He had called across an arm of the lake that ran up into the lava beds that he had more wounded men that he could take care of. Gen. Wheaton was now thoroughly distressed, saying "when Bernard hallows he is badly hurt." We then determined to try shelling the Indians with the howitzers and I started back to find the pack mules. Reader, if you ever tried to appear as if you weren't scared, with bullets screaming around you, and with your back to the enemy, you will know something of my feelings. Those big fellows, striking in the rocks would glance and scream with an unearthly noise. My legs wanted to run, but pride held them in check. And right here I want to say, that bravery is only pride and a good control over your legs. I finally found the pack mules and started back, but it wasn't half as hard facing it and we came bravely up to the line. The guns were planted and opened with shells timed to three hundred yards. Two burst and a call came from Bernard's men that we were shelling their rear guard.

Firing with the howitzers ceased as it was clearly a failure, and a consultation was held. We knew our loss was heavy, Gen. Ross declaring it "is worse than Hungry Hill." It was finally determined to send a column to relieve Col. Bernard. Accordingly Fairchild's California volunteers, Mason's battalion and Perry's dismounted cavalry were ordered to cut their way around the lake shore and join Bernard. Fairchild's men passed over the point without loss, but several of Mason's men were killed in plain sight. The soldiers balked and refused to advance. Col. Green ran down the line and leaping upon the point turned his back to the Indians and with a gauntlet in his hand used language that was scarcely fit for a parlour. Gen. Wheaton also joined and with a sword taken from a bugler boy, ran down the line urging the men to move forward. They soon began the advance and passed over the point and out of sight. Meantime I was moving the volunteers down towards the lake to take the places in our front vacated by the relief column. The battle now became desperate, the Indians concentrating all their forces against the column going round the lake. In this situation the volunteers pressed forward and soon we could hear the women and children crying. Applegate's men were almost on top of them and were getting into camp. We were within 50 yards of the scalp pole over Jack's cave which was the centre of the stronghold. The volunteers were anxious to charge. I went back to where Gen. Wheaton was standing and explaining the situation asked permission to charge with all the volunteers. The fog had raised and Capt. Adams of the signal staff was signalling to Bernard. I told Gen. Wheaton if he would have Bernard cease firing I would charge and close the Indians out in twenty minutes, that our men were on top of them.

The General walked rapidly back and forth, snapping his fingers for a few moments, and then turning to me exclaimed: "You can go, but not with my consent. We have lost too many men already—five times more than Jackson lost at New Orleans. The country will not justify this sacrifice of human life. You have taken these young men and boys off the farms and from stores, schools and shops and their lives are worth something to their families and to their country. You can go but not with my consent." Then turning to Gen. Ross, who had scarcely spoken a word during the day, he said: "General, what had we better, do?"

"We had better get out of here, by God," exclaimed the bluff old veteran.

"All right, Capt. Adams, tell Bernard that as soon as the relief column reaches him to hold his position until dark and then withdraw," exclaimed Wheaton in rapid succession. Then turning to me he said: "Colonel, we will have to depend on the volunteers to protect our wounded and mule train in getting out of this place."

It was soon arranged that the men were to keep firing until dark and then begin the retreat. Just after sundown Bernard signalled that the relief column had reached him, but there is not a question of doubt had not the volunteers pressed the Indians so hard at a critical time Fairchild's, Mason's and Perry's command would have been annihilated. Jud Small was badly wounded in the shoulder and afterwards told me that he was shot by an Indian not twenty feet away. At one point the men lay in the water and rolled over and over with only their heads exposed.

Night finally closed in and with the gathering darkness the fog rolled in from the lake, increasing its intensity. Kelley's company was formed in the rear with Applegate's company on the flank, and formed parallel with the lake, along the shores of which we were to make our way, with the wounded men on litters between. Finally the word was passed along the lines to move forward. The night had meanwhile settled down to one of Stygean blackness. Objects a foot away were indistinguishable, and we had to feel rather than see our way. I fully realized the difficulties and dangers of our situation, but my anxiety was for the nineteen wounded men on the litters. I told Col. Bellinger that we must remain together and behind the litter bearers, that I would rather leave my body with our dead comrades in the rocks than to leave behind any of our wounded men. But we had proceeded but a short distance when the lines crumbled and became mixed up, in fact, an undistinguishable mob. Under these circumstances, and relying on undisciplined troops, our position was critical in the extreme. One shot would have precipitated a stampede. Wheaton, Ross and Miller were somewhere mixed up among the troops, but Bellinger and I stuck to the litter bearers and kept as many of the men behind us as possible.

Donald McKay's Indians were in the advance, somewhere, but we knew not where. In this order, or rather disorder, we stumbled along blindly, knowing the waters of the lake were on our right. The bottom of the bluff was finally reached and word passed back that the Modocs had captured and held the summit. I stopped as many of the men as possible and asked Col. Bellinger to remain with the litter bearers and I would go forward and if necessary capture it back. Reaching the front I found Indians, volunteers and officers all jumbled together without semblance of order. The Indians were confident the Modocs had killed the guards left there in the morning and held the top of the bluff. I called for volunteers, but not an Indian would go. I finally got a few volunteers and began the ascent of the steep, rocky trail. The climb was tedious in the extreme, and one can imagine my joy when on nearing the crest there came the sharp call, "Who comes there?" I was prompt to reply "friends." Learning that all was well, I retraced my steps to the bottom and gave out the welcome news that everything was clear.

Then began a scramble to reach the top. It was everybody for himself, as it was too dark to even attempt to preserve a semblance of order or discipline. Going to the rear I found Col. Bellinger with the wounded men. Holding as many men as possible we began the ascent. As the litter bearers gave out others took their places and the tired men slipped away in the darkness. As we neared the top, Col. Bellinger and I relieved two worn out bearers and that was the last we saw of them. In this condition we staggered into camp at 2 o'clock in the morning, more dead than alive. To add to the discomfort of the situation others had reached our store of provisions ahead of us, and we simply had to do without. We had now been on the march 24 hours. Our boot soles were almost cut away on the sharp lava, and we were all but barefooted. But I had my horse, and though I had nothing to eat, I felt greatly relieved. A few hours sleep on the frozen ground and we were again astir. I was holding my horse to graze when Gen. Wheaton's orderly came to me and stated that the General wanted to see me at his tent. Handing him the halter strap I walked down to the tent and stepped in. The General was sitting on the ground with a can of coffee before him. He said he had a couple of cups of coffee and four crackers and wanted to divide with me. It required no persuasion on his part to induce me to accept.

While we were sipping our coffee we discussed the events of the previous day. The General was visibly affected and greatly worried. Even then we did not know the full extent of our losses. The dead were left where they fell and only our wounded carried out. Would the country justify the sacrifice of life, not knowing the character of the country over which we had fought? Speaking of the lava beds, the General remarked: "I have seen something of war and know something of fortifications. I commanded 19,000 men at the battle of the Wilderness and saw many of the great engineering works of the Civil war, but I do not believe that a hundred thousand men in a hundred thousand years could construct such fortifications." This will give the reader a faint idea of the lava beds. Indeed a regiment of men could conceal themselves in its caves and fissures and ten thousand men could be marched over them without seeing a man.

Placing the wounded in ambulances we now broke camp and started to our camp at Van Bremer's ranch. After a tiresome march by way of Lower Klamath Lake, the wounded men undergoing terrible sufferings, we reached camp at 11 o'clock that night. Here another difficulty confronted us. Our provision train had not arrived and we were reduced to beef straight. There was some murmuring among the men, kept up and agitated by a doctor attached to Kelley's company who told the men that they had been robbed and swindled by the officers. Hearing of this I hunted him up. He said that a "soldier did not dare to complain without being called a son-of-a-b——."

Twenty or thirty volunteers were standing around. I explained that the wagons had been two weeks on the road; that they had made only ten miles in seven days; and that a man, private or officer who would talk about asking for his discharge, though all were entitled to the same, was a son of a b—h, and a d—d one at that. He went to Gen. Ross and complained of my language, but was told that the "Colonel knew what he was talking about."

The disgruntled pill mixer mounted his horse and left, and that was the last we heard about being discharged. We continued feasting on beef straight and fattened on the diet, at least I did.

The day after our return we buried the man I had seen shot through the stomach, while crawling on his belly. Patrick Maher was buried with military honours. On the fourth day the troops sent to relieve Col. Bernard arrived at camp, and the reports all being in we found that 41 men had been killed in the fighting on the 16th and 17th of January. The death of Patrick Maher made 42, besides a long list of wounded. When we consider that there were not more than 500 engaged, counting McKay's Indians, the loss was heavy, and would the Government endorse or censure the officers, was the question.

As before stated, we were camped at the ranch of Van Bremer Bros. On our return Col. Bellinger and I had to give up our quarters in an outhouse to accommodate the wounded men and after that we slept, when we slept at all, on the frozen ground with two thicknesses of blanket beneath us. Under such circumstances it may easily be imagined that our periods of sleep were of short duration. We would drop asleep and in an hour wake up shivering. We would get up, cut off some beef and roast it before the fires that were constantly kept burning, get warm and then lie down again. I mention this, not because we were undergoing hardships more trying than others, but to show how all, officers and men, fared. There was no difference. One day a surgeon came to me and asked if I could obtain some eggs for the wounded men, so I went to Van Bremer and got half a dozen eggs and paid 50 cents each for them. He would not take script but demanded and received the cash, nearly all I had. From that time until our departure I spent a considerable portion of my time in studying human villainy with the Van Bremers as a model. But I got even with them—and then some. Before leaving I asked Gen. Ross for permission to settle our hay bill in place of the Quartermaster, Mr. Foudray. Capt. Adams and I then measured the hay used respectively by the regulars and volunteers, and I feel safe in saying that those eggs cost the Van Bremer Bros. $50 each.

Of course they raved and ranted, declaring that we were worse than the Modocs, but when they saw the tents of the regulars and blankets of the volunteers being pulled down and rolled up they came to me and asked what it meant. I told them that we had been ordered to the mouth of Lost River on Tule Lake to protect the Oregon settlers, and that the regulars were going also, but that Gen. Wheaton was going to leave a detail at the Fairchilds ranch and that if they did not feel safe with the Modocs they could move up there. They lost no time in loading a few effects into a wagon and started with us to the Fairchilds ranch. On the road they mired down and every man, regular and volunteer, passing them had something bitter and mean to say to them. The story of the eggs was known to all, and if ever men paid for a scurvy, mean trick it was the Van Bremers.

We moved around to Lost River and struck camp, where we remained about ten days. As Gen. Wheaton felt competent to protect the settlements, and as the term of enlistment of the volunteers had expired more than a month before, we proceeded to Linkville and from there to Jacksonville where the command of Capt. Kelley was disbanded, Applegate's company having been discharged at Linkville. I then returned to Salem and a few days later paid a visit to Gen. Canby at Ft. Vancouver in company with Governor L. F. Grover. The entire situation was gone over, Gen. Canby expressing entire confidence in the ability of Gen. Wheaton and his officers. Fortunate, indeed, would it have been had that brave officer and splendid gentleman been left to develop and carry out his plans, but unhappily that was not to be, for the churches succeeded in hypnotizing the grim soldier in the White House, and the result was the "Peace Commission."

CHAPTER 12

The Peace Commission's Work

A. B. Meacham was at that time in Washington. He had been superseded as Superintendent of Indian Affairs by T. B. Odeneal. Meacham wanted the place, and backed by the churches and humanitarians of New England, thought he could accomplish his purpose by means of a compromise with Jack and his band. He declared to President Grant that he knew Jack to be an honourable man and that he could easily effect a compromise and induce the outlaws to return to the reservation. Meantime a clamour went up all over the country, especially in the east. Sentimentalists shed barrels of tears over the wrongs of the Indians, the horrors of the Ben Wright massacre were recapitulated with all manner of untruthful variations, and the great Beecher from the pulpit of his Brooklyn tabernacle sent up a prayer for "that poor, persecuted people whose long pent up wrongs had driven them to acts of outrage and diabolical murder." Delegations, at the instigation of Meacham, visited the White House and finally succeeded in bending the iron will of the grim old soldier to their own. The hands that slew the Bodys and Brothertons were to be clasped in a spirit of brotherly love, and the principles and precepts of the "Lowly Nazarene" were to be extended to these gentle butchers.

Accordingly in February a commission was appointed

consisting of A. B. Meacham, Jesse Applegate, and S. Case. The commission arrived at headquarters towards the last of February. They were instructed by the Commissioner of Indian Affairs "to ascertain the causes which led to hostilities between the Modocs and the U. S. troops;" to offer them a reservation somewhere on the coast with immunity for past crimes.

In vain Gov. Grover of Oregon protested against any compromise with the murderers of Oregon citizens. He held that they were amenable to the laws of that State, had been indicted by a grand jury, and should be tried and executed as the law directs, but his protest was passed unheeded and the commissioners proceeded to carry out their instructions. Bob Whittle and his Indian wife were sent to convey the terms to Capt. Jack and his band, but Jack refused to have anything to do with the commissioners, although willing to talk to Judges Roseborough and Steele of Yreka. These gentlemen proceeded to the camp in the lava beds and held a conference and found that Jack was anxious for peace; was tired of war; did not know the commissioners; but wanted to talk to the chief soldiers, Generals Canby and Gillem.

The former had arrived and assumed command of the one thousand or more troops assembled, while the latter had superseded Gen. Wheaton. John Fairchilds also had an interview with them in the lava beds and was only saved from massacre by one of the Indians, who kept him in his cave all night and escorted him beyond the lines the next morning. After some weeks of delay Jack finally agreed to a conference with the commissioners, but the terms were such as to leave no doubt of intended treachery, and Mr. Applegate and Mr. Case resigned in disgust. It was apparent to these men that the Indians only sought an opportunity to murder Gen. Canby and such other officers as they could get into their power, but Meacham was determined to succeed, as that was the only means of getting back his job as Superintendent of Indian Affairs. Accordingly Rev. Dr. Thomas of Oakland

and Mr. Dyer, Indian agent at Klamath, were appointed to fill the vacancies.

In the meantime Gen. Canby had moved his headquarters to the foot of the bluff at the lower end of Tule Lake, while Col. John Green with Mason's command had moved down from Land's ranch to a position within striking distance of the stronghold. Five mortars and three howitzers with an abundance of ammunition and provisions were also moved up to the front.

But the dreary farce was not to be ended yet. On April 10th four bucks and five squaws rode into Gen. Canby's camp. They were fed and clothed by the commission, loaded with presents, and sent back asking for a conference between the lines. Later in the day Bogus Charley, the Umpqua, came into camp and surrendering his gun, stated that he would not return. He remained in camp over night and in the morning was joined by "Boston Charley," one of the leaders who stated that Capt. Jack was willing to meet the commissioners midway between the lines on the condition that Jack was to be attended by four of his men, all unarmed. Boston then mounted his horse and rode away. Bogus accompanying him.

A tent had been pitched midway between the lines and thither Commissioners Meacham, Thomas, and Dyer, and Gen. Canby repaired accompanied by Frank Riddle and his Modoc wife as interpreters. Before starting both Riddle and his squaw in vain tried to dissuade the commissioners from their purpose. Meacham told Gen. Canby that Riddle only sought to delay negotiations in order to prolong his job as interpreter; that he knew Capt. Jack and that he "was an honourable man." Rev. Mr. Thomas when appealed to by Riddle replied that he "was in the hands of his God." Both Riddle and his squaw then, at the suggestion of Mr. Dyer, went to the tent of Gen. Canby and begged him not to go. With tears streaming down her cheeks the woman implored the General not to go, as treachery was surely meditated. Gen. Canby replied that "his Government had ordered him to go, and a soldier had no choice but to obey orders." The General was dressed in full uniform, with sword belt and empty scabbard.

Gen. Gillem intended to accompany them but was too indisposed to leave his tent. Riddle, in describing what transpired at the "peace tent," told me that Meacham made a short speech and was followed by Dr. Thomas and Gen. Canby. Capt. Jack then made a speech, demanding Hot Creek and Cottonwood as a reservation, owned at that time by the Dorris brothers, Fairchilds and Doten. Meacham then explained to him the impossibility of acceding to his demands, as the property had already passed in title to these men. Old Sconchin then told Meacham to "shut up;" that he had said enough. While Sconchin was talking Jack got up and was walking behind the others. He then turned back and exclaimed: "All ready!" At the same instant he drew a pistol and snapped at Gen. Canby, but cocking the pistol again shot him through the right eye. Canby fell dead without a groan. Almost at the same instant Sconchin shot Meacham through the shoulder, in the head and in the arm, while Boston Charley shot Dr. Thomas dead. Just previous to the shooting Mr. Dyer had turned and walked back behind the tent. At the first crack of the pistols Mr. Dyer fled for his life, closely pursued by Hooker Jim. Mr. Dyer had concealed a small revolver about his person and turned at intervals of his flight and fired at his pursuer. By this means he was enabled to make headway. and at last escaped.

Gen. Canby and Dr. Thomas were stripped and the General scalped. Meacham was insensible and as the Indians started in to scalp him Riddle's squaw told them that the soldiers were coming, and they left him and fled. To this fact Meacham was indebted for his scalp, as it was partly cut loose and in a few moments more would have been stripped off.

While these scenes were being enacted, two Indians approached the lines of Mason and Green bearing a flag of truce. Lieutenants Sherwood and Boyle went out about 500 yards beyond their line to meet them. The Indians said they wanted to see Maj. Mason and when told by the officers that Mason would not talk to them, they appeared disappointed. As the officers turned to go back to their lines they were fired upon by Indians in ambush and Lieut. Sherwood was mortally wounded.

Early in the day Capt. Adams had been stationed on Gillem's bluff and during all the proceedings at the peace tent had watched with a strong field glass. When the massacre of the commission began he telegraphed to Gen. Gillem, and the soldiers, held in readiness for an emergency, sprang to the advance on the double quick, but were too late to save the life of the gallant Canby and his comrades.

Thus ended the long, dreary farce of the "Peace Commission." And at what a price! There lay the noble Canby prone upon his face, cold and still in death; having breasted the hurricane of many a well-fought field to fall at last by the treacherous, assassin hand of a prowling savage to whom he had come upon a mission of peace and friendship. There was another of the Commissioners, a man of peace, a preacher of the gospel of eternal love, stricken down with the words of mercy and forgiveness upon his lips, his gray and reverend locks all dabbled in his own blood. Another, shot and hacked and stabbed, covered with wounds, beaten down with cruel blows, motionless but still alive. And there was another, with war-whoop and pistol shot ringing at his heels, fleeing for his life; while at the side scene was the "honourable" Capt. Jack, stage manager of the awful play, arch demon of massacre, with pistol that took the priceless life of Canby still smoking in his hand, leaping with glee, his dark face all aglow with the glare of the dread spectacle, like a fiend dancing in the fire-light of hell.

No wonder that in its lurid light the Government for a moment forgot its dawdling "peace policy," and "let slip the dogs of war." No wonder the canting prayers of maudlin fanatics were stilled amid the wrathful cry for vengeance. The blood of Canby and Thomas and Sherwood "cried unto God from the ground" against them. The ghastly, sickening tragedy which should send a thrill through the very heart of the nation was consummated.

CHAPTER 13

Three Days' Battle in the Lava Beds

The day following the massacre preparations were made for an attack in full force upon the stronghold. Only the regulars were to be engaged in this task, as the volunteers had been discharged, under assurance from Gen. Canby that he was strong enough to control the situation and protect the settlements. The plan of battle which was the same as that adopted by Gen. Wheaton on the 17th of January was to form a cordon of troops around the hostiles and either kill or capture them. The troops were supplied with over-coats, blankets, three days' provisions and an abundance of ammunition.

On April 13, Donald McKay arrived with seventy-two Wasco Indians who were at once armed and assigned to duty, and who made a splendid record. Some slight skir-mishing had taken place, but no general forward movement was made until the 14th, when the rattle of small arms, the yells of the savages, and the deep boom of the mortars and howitzers told that the battle was on. All day long the troops continued to advance, slowly, keeping under cover as much as possible, and driving the Indians before them. Even with every precaution there was a list of killed and wounded. As night closed in the troops held their position, but the mortars and howitzers continued to send into the stronghold a stream of shells, mingled with the occasional discharge of small arms and the yells of the savages.

During the night Col. Green and Maj. Mason, disobeying orders (I know what I am saying) drove a column in between the Indians and the lake, thus shutting them off from water. This was carrying out the plans formulated and advised by Gen. Wheaton and Gen. Ross after the battle on the 17th of January. When the Indians discovered this move they made a determined attempt to break the line, but the troops had had time to fortify and the attempt proved a failure.

Gen. Gillem the next morning sent for John Fairchilds and asked him to go with Capt. Bancroft and show him where to plant the mortars and also show him the centre of the stronghold. Fairchilds told the General that he would show him, but that he was tired acting as errand boy for Tom, Dick and Harry—that he had risked his life enough. Under these circumstances, the General had to go. They started out and had almost reached the line, bullets were singing around, when the General, rubbing his hands, remarked:

"Mr. Fairchilds, this is a splendid day's work; how long did it take Gen. Wheaton to get this far?"

Fairchilds, as brave a man as ever trod in shoe leather, replied: "General, I do not remember exactly, but as near as I can judge it was about twenty minutes."

That remark settled the friendly relations between the two men. I want to say here that Gillem was not the man for the place. He was self-willed, self-opinionated, knew nothing about Indian warfare; in fact, got his shoulder straps through the enterprise of one of his officers and the treachery of a woman, in killing the Confederate Gen. Morgan. He had nothing else to recommend him, and would not take advice from old veterans like Green, Mason, Bernard, Perry and Hasbrook—men who had grown gray in frontier service.

At 9 o'clock on the morning of the second day, Col. Green

ordered an advance. The men answered with a cheer, and soon reached a position on top of the ridge next to Jack's camp. Some of the other lines also slowly advanced during the day. Towards evening another desperate attempt was made by the Indians to break the line between them and water. At this time a very near approach to a battle was reached. Volley after volley of rifles rang out, and mingled with the yells of the savages and roar of the artillery made some of the old veterans of the Civil War think they were really in a fight. All the same, men were being killed and others wounded, even though there was no battle.

Col. Green realized that if the Indians could be kept from the water, they would have to surrender or leave the stronghold, and he held on with the tenacity of a bulldog. During the night the squaws went out under the lines and returned with a load of snow, but the warm spell of weather melted the snow rapidly and soon this source was cut off. Still the outlaws held on, and for three days and nights, pressed in by men and guns on every side, subjected to a fire from four sides, with five mortars and three howitzers raining shells upon them, they held to the "hole in the wall" that had been for ages their salvation and their safeguard. The constant rain of bursting shells had filled the caves and crevices of the lava beds with smoke, and cut off from water, on the night of the third day they quietly slipped out from under Gen. Gillem's lines and left—no one knew where.

It may appear incredible, but it is true, that during all this battle of three days and nights, amid the hum of tons of leaden bullets and the bursting of countless shells, not a single Indian was killed. We must except one buck who started in to investigate an unexploded shell. That buck was going to "get 'um powder and lead out" with file and hatchet, and was scattered out over the rocks for his inquisitiveness. But the other Indians were nowhere to be seen. They had passed out under the line of troops as ants would pass through a sponge.

113

The troops took possession of the lava beds, the stronghold, but the Indians were gone. It yet remained for Gen. Gillem to learn another lesson in Indian warfare.

When the news was received by Gov. Grover that the Indians had left the stronghold and that the settlers were again exposed, he ordered out two companies of volunteers, one from Douglas county under Capt. Rodgers and the other from Jackson county under Capt. Hizer. I was not ordered at the time to accompany the volunteers, the "mad-cap from Salem" was to be left behind, but not for long. In spite of the abuse of enemies, mostly those fellows who sought safety with women and children behind strong stockades, and the declaration of Mr. Meacham that I was responsible for the slaughter of men on the 17th of January, "when the brave, reckless, madcap, Col. Thompson, drove his men against the lines of the Modocs," I was again sent to the front. In my letters and newspaper articles I had severely censured Mr. Meacham and he took revenge in his *Wigwam and Warpath* by declaring the mad-cap was to blame for the slaughter. I never met him but once after the close of the war and that was in the library of the old Russ House in San Francisco, where I had gone to call upon a couple of friends. This was in August after the close of the war. He was walking back and forth in the library, his head yet bandaged where the Indians had started to scalp him, when he suddenly turned and said:

"Col. Thompson. I want to speak to you."

I excused myself to Rollin P. Saxe, one of my friends, and walked up to Mr. Meacham. He said:

"I had made up my mind to shoot you on sight." Then hesitating an instant, continued, "but I have changed my mind."

"Perhaps," I replied, "Mr. Meacham, it is fortunate for you or I that you have changed your mind." He then went on to detail how I had abused him. I said, "Mr. Meacham, before God, you are responsible for the death of Gen. Canby, a noble man and soldier, and I don't know how many others."

After conversing some time we separated, never to meet again.

But to return to the war. On the 18th Gen. Gillem sent out Col. Thomas and Major Wright on a scouting expedition in the lava region to discover if possible the whereabouts of the savages. The scouting party numbered sixty-two men, including Lieutenants Cranston, Harve, and Harris. Instead of sending out experienced men, these men were sent to be slaughtered, as the result demonstrated. Gillem was not only incompetent personally, but was jealous of every man, citizen or regular, who was competent. The party scouted around through the lava for a distance of several miles. They saw no Indians or sign of Indians. The hostiles had fled and were nowhere to be found. They sat down to eat their lunch. They were quietly surrounded and at the first fire the soldiers, as is almost always the case, became panic stricken. The officers bravely strove to stem the tide of panic, but hopelessly. The panic became a rout and the rout a massacre, and of the sixty-two men who were sent out that morning but two were alive, and they were desperately wounded.

Had any one of the old experienced officers, like Green, Mason, Perry, Bernard or Hasbrook been sent on this duty a massacre would have been impossible. They would never have been caught off their guard and the sickening massacre would have been averted. The very fact of no Indians in sight would have taught these men caution.

The entire command of Gen. Gillem now became demoralized, and desertions were by the wholesale. Gen. Gillem fortified his camp at the foot of the bluff, and surrounded it with a rock wall. His communications were cut off and his trains captured and destroyed. "Gillem's Camp" was a fort as well as a "graveyard." Trains of wagons were captured, the wagons burned and the animals taken away. The Indians daily fired on his picket line.

Such was the deplorable conditions of affairs when Gen.

Jeff C. Davis assumed command. Davis was eminently fitted for the task assigned him. He at once restored confidence among the disheartened and beaten men. He declared if there was to be more massacres he would know who to blame, and led the scouting parties in person. The camp at "Gillem's Graveyard" was broken up, and leaving a force to hold the stronghold he began scouting and searching for the enemy. He went with six men to search for traces of the hostiles. His action restored confidence, and the men manifested a spirit of fight. Donald McKay and his Wascos were sent to circle the lava beds. That night his signal fires informed Gen. Davis that the Modocs had deserted the lava beds. All available cavalry were sent in pursuit. The command of Capt. Hasbrook had been out all day, and was accompanied by Donald McKay's Indians. Arriving at Dry Lake, then politely called Sauress Lake, they found that there was no water. Wells were dug but to no purpose, and McKay and his Indians were sent back to Boyles' camp for water.

From Dry Lake to Boyles' camp the distance was about twelve miles. With a pack train McKay was in no hurry; as a matter of fact, Donald was never in a hurry when there was danger about. He was a coward, but had some brave men of the Wascos with him. I speak advisedly of what I know.

Capt. Hasbrook's command went into camp feeling secure, as the Indians were in hiding. But Hasbrook, old soldier as he was, had a lesson to learn. During the night a dog, belonging to the packers, kept growling. The boss of the train, Charley Larengel, went to the officer of the guard and told him the Indians were about and that they would certainly be attacked at daylight. Mr. Larengel told me that the officer treated his advice with indifference, not to say contempt. The "boss of the pack train was unduly alarmed, there were no Indians around." But Charley Larengel knew a thing or two. He had been with Crook and knew that hostiles did not come out, shake their red blankets and dare the soldiers to a fight, so he barricaded his camp, using the *apparajos* as breast works and told the packers to "let the mules go to the devil. We must look out for ourselves."

Just as day began to break over the desolate hills, the fun began. From three sides the Indians poured into the camp a withering fire. As a result the entire command became panic stricken. Seven men were knocked down, almost at the first fire, and it has always been a matter of surprise to me that Hasbrook, old campaigner as he was, should be caught off his guard. It began to look like another Wright-Thomas massacre. Captain Jack stood well out of harm's way, dressed in the uniform of Gen. Canby, and giving orders. It was surely another massacre.

But the Modocs had not seen Donald McKay and his Wascos leave the camp the evening before, nor were they aware that he was within striking distance that morning, at a most critical time. Hearing the firing and yells McKay left his pack animals, and under the leadership of Captain George, chief of the Wascos, attacked the Modocs in the rear.

From a rout of the soldiers it became a rout of the Modocs. They quickly fled and Jack was the first man to run. This brought on dissensions, for the Hot Creeks claimed they had to do all the fighting, all the guard duty, had, in fact, to endure all the hardships, while old Jack in his gold braided uniform stood at a safe distance giving orders. During the dispute Hooker Jim shot at, or attempted to shoot Jack.

The Modocs, or renegades were now out of the lava beds, and with soldiers and volunteers practically surrounding them, and with dissensions in their own camp, the band broke up. Jack and his band went in a northeast direction, closely followed by Hasbrook and McKay's Indians, and two days later surrendered.

The Hot Creeks went around the lower end of Tule Lake and surrendered to Gen. Davis at the Fairchilds-Doten ranch. Hooker Jim, followed them and seeing they were not massacred by the soldiers, determined to surrender. Yet this Indian, one of the worst of the band of outlaws, was an outlaw to every human being on earth. He dared not go to Jack's band, his own party had disowned and tried to kill him. He watched the band from the bald hills above the ranch enter the camp of the soldiers. He saw they were not massacred. He then made up his mind to surrender. He fixed in his mind the tent of Gen. Davis. Crawling as close to the line of pickets as possible, he raised his gun above his head and yelling "Me Hooker Jim," ran through the lines, among soldiers, and up to the tent door of Gen. Davis, threw down his gun, and said, "me Hooker Jim, I give up."

In speaking of the surrender, Gen. Davis said to me: "Here was a man, an outlaw to every human being on earth, throwing down his rifle and saying, "me Hooker Jim, me give up." He stood before me as stolid as a bronze. I have seen some grand sights, but taking everything into consideration, that was the grandest sight I ever witnessed."

Hasbrook followed relentlessly Jack's band and captured them in the canyon below Steel Swamp. Jack was an arrant coward, but old Sconchin, whose bows and arrows I retain as a souvenir, and which were presented to me by a sergeant of the troop, was a fighter, and would have died fighting.

CHAPTER 14

Trailing the Fugitives

While all this was going on I was riding from Salem, Oregon, "Gov. Grover's mad-cap Colonel," as Jas. D. Fay, Harvey Scott of the Oregonian, and some other of my enemies, designated me. Fay did not like me and I happened to be with Senator Nesmith when he caned Harvey Scott in the Chemeketa Hotel at Salem. My meeting with Senator Nesmith was accidental, but Scott never forgave me, nor did he in fact neglect any opportunity to "lambaste" me after that time.

But to return to my trip. The Oregon volunteers had been ordered out, with General Ross in command. The murderers of the 17 settlers along the shores of Tule Lake had been indicted by the Grand jury of Jackson County, Oregon. The Governor demanded the surrender of the murderers from the United States authorities. The murderers were not yet captured but we knew it was only a matter of days. I left Salem on Thursday and went by train to Roseburg that evening. There I took the stage, and telegraphing ahead for horses at Jacksonville found a magnificent saddle horse awaiting me. Did you ever travel from Salem to Roseburg by train and then by stage to Jacksonville through the long weary night?

If so you will have some faint idea of my condition. Arriving at Jacksonville I lost no time in proceeding on my journey. That night I rode to Coldwells' place, sometimes called the Soda Springs. The next morning at 4 o'clock, after only about 4 hours' rest in 48, I started on my journey. I knew how to ride a horse, how to save him and how to rest him. At the head of "Green Springs" I met a Government courier. He told me that Gen. Ross had left Linkville that morning with his entire command.

Thanking the courier, I then began to ride, and at precisely half past 11 o'clock was shaking hands with Alex Miller at Linkville. I had ridden one horse 55 miles that morning over a range of mountains. Mr. Miller asked me, when did you leave Salem?"

"Day before yesterday noon," I replied.

"If I did not have all kinds of respect for you I would call you a liar" remarked Mr. Miller. Just them J. B. Neil and Mr. Jackson, District Attorney and Sheriff of Jackson County came up, and showing these gentlemen my papers with the dates, stopped all further discussion of the matter. But I said, "Alex, I want the best horse in Linkville, for I am going to overtake Gen. Ross tonight."

"You shall have not only the best horse in Linkville, but the best horse in the State of Oregon." A ride of 45 miles that evening accompanied by Mr. Neil and Mr. Jackson, convinced me that Alex. Miller told me the truth. We reached the headquarters of Gen. Ross late in the night. I had ridden that day 95 miles on two horses, and I want here to plead guilty to cruelty to animals. The horse I rode into Linkville, to use the common expression, "quit," and the only means I could use to get a "move on," was to shoot the tips of his ears off with my revolver. I will say further that this is the only instance in my life when I was cruel to a dumb brute, but I justified myself then and now on the grounds of "Duty."

Arriving at Headquarters, "for the night," as the General expressed it, the next morning we took up the trail of a band of Jack's renegades. Black Jim, one of the worst of the band of murderers, headed the band. There were only about twenty men in the outfit, and the only means we had of following them was by a crutch used by an Indian shot by John Fairchilds on the 17th of January. Late one evening, in fact just at sundown, we lost the trail. We had tracked the stick to a juniper tree, but there lost it. Finally one of our boys discovered a hand up in the juniper and levelling his gun, told him to come down.

After some parley the Indian came down. Gen. Ross and I told him we were chiefs and that all Indians surrendering would be protected. A hundred yards away, somewhere between Tule Lake and Langel Valley, there was a rim rock, and in this the Indians were hiding. On assurance from our juniper tree man they finally surrendered. Only Black Jim showed any hesitancy, but the muzzle of a 50 calibre Springfield answered as a magnificent persuader.

We then returned to Tule Lake, sending for Mrs. Body and Mrs. Schira to identify the murderers of their families. We were still on the Oregon side of the line, but much to our disappointment neither of the ladies could identify any of the men. We had Black Jim but the ladies did not and could not identify him. We therefore took them to the headquarters of Gen. Davis and surrendered them at the Peninsula.

We arrived about 10 o'clock. I went to the tent of Gen. Wheaton and told him my business. Mr. Neil and Mr. Jackson were with me. Gen. Wheaton took us up to the tent of Gen. Davis and introduced us. I presented to Gen. Davis my papers and told him that the officers of the law were there. The General replied, as nearly as I can remember, "Colonel, I will deliver them to you at any time after 2 o'clock, at least, I will deliver to you their bodies." I simply replied, "that is entirely satisfactory, both to the officers present, the Governor of Oregon and to your humble servant."

He then told me that he had the timbers all framed and ready to put together and intended to hang all the murderers promptly at 2 o'clock.

While we were talking a courier arrived with dispatches

from the Secretary of War instructing him to hold the murderers until further orders. All were astounded, but a soldier has no choice but to obey orders. Gen. Davis was angry, and remarked to me that if he "had any way of making a living for his family outside of the army he would resign today."

Mrs. Body, Mrs. Schira, Mrs. Brotherton were all there. Their entire families had been wiped out-butchered. The Indians took a large amount of jewellery, pictures, and more than $4,000 in money. A tent had been spread for the ladies and Gen. Davis had ordered a tent, with tables, chairs, bed, writing material, etc., arranged for my convenience. The correspondent of the *New York Herald* was living at the sutler's tent, in fact, with good old Pat McManus.

Mrs. Body and Mrs. Schira had also been provided with a tent. They sent to Gen. Davis and asked that they be permitted to talk with Black Jim, Hooker Jim and one or two others. They said that possibly some of the family relics could be reclaimed. The order was issued and the General and I were talking of the awful results of the war and its blunders.

Suddenly Fox of the *New York Herald* called at the door of Gen. Davis' tent and said, "the women are going to kill the Indians." Both of us sprang from the tent door and rushed to the tent where the women were domiciled. Davis was ahead of me. I saw Mrs. Schira with a double edged knife poised. Hooker Jim was standing fronting the women, as stolid as a bronze. Mrs. Schira's mother was attempting to cock a revolver. Gen. Davis made a grab for the knife, catching the blade in his right hand and in the struggle his hand was badly lacerated. A surgeon was called who dressed the wounded hand, and then we all went to dinner at "Boyles' mess." At the dinner table were seated about forty officers, men grown gray in the service of their country and young Lieutenants just out from West Point. The latter, as is always the case, were in full uniform, while the old fellows wore little or nothing that would indicate their calling or rank. During dinner one of the young men made some slighting remark about the conduct of the women in attempting to kill the Indians, characterizing their act as unwarranted and a breach of respect to the General.

Instantly Gen. Davis pushed back from the table and rose to feet, fire flashing from his eyes, and if ever a young upstart received a lecture that young officer received one. I was sitting to the left of Gen. Davis while Jesse Applegate, one of the "Makers of Oregon," sat at his right. The General spoke of the women as the wife and daughter of a frontiersman, and before whom stood the bloody handed butcher of husbands and sons. It was one of the most eloquent, at the same time one of the most withering addresses that it has ever been my fortune to hear. Resuming his seat the General continued his conversation with those about him, but there were no more remarks, you may be assured, upon this incident.

The next morning at daylight the orderly to Gen. Davis came to my tent and awaking me said that the General wanted to see me at once. Hastily dressing I walked over to the General's tent. He was sitting on the side of his camp bed, partly undressed. Jas. Fairchilds was sitting in the tent talking as I entered. The General asked him to repeat to me what he had been saying. Mr. Fairchilds then proceeded to relate that a bunch of Indians, four bucks and a lot of women and children, had come in to the ranch and surrendered. He had loaded them into a wagon and started to the Peninsula to turn them over to the military authorities. When within about six miles of his destination he was headed off by two men who were disguised past identification. They ordered him to stop and unhitch his team and after doing so was told to drive the horses up the road. When about thirty yards away he was ordered to stop. The men then began killing the Indians while he stood looking on and holding to his team. After firing a dozen shots into the wagon, the men rode away, telling him to remain there and not to leave. He remained until dark and then mounting one of his horses rode to camp.

While we were talking Donald McKay came up and accused the volunteers of the massacre. I told Gen. Davis that it was impossible that the volunteers could have committed the crime. McKay was drunk and swaggered around a great deal and finally asked the General to let him take his Indians and follow the volunteers and bring them back.

Becoming angered at the talk and swagger of McKay I told the General to let him go, and plainly told McKay that I would go with him. That he, McKay, was an arrant coward and could not take any one, much less a company of one hundred men. I then expressed my belief to Gen. Davis that the killing had been done by some of the settlers whose relatives had been massacred by the savages; that Gen. Ross had gone around the south end of the lake and that Capt. Hizer must have been many miles on his road towards Linkville.

I told him, however, that I would make an investigation and if possible bring the perpetrators of the act to justice. Mounting my horse I rode rapidly back to where the wagon was standing in the road. The women and children were still in the wagon with their dead, not one of them having moved during the night. It was a most ghastly sight, the blood from the dead Indians had run through the wagon bed, and made a broad, red streak for twenty yards down the road. Soon after my arrival Donald McKay rode up, and I ordered him to go to the lake and get some water for the women, one of whom had been severely wounded. Soon after his return with the water Mr. Fairchilds came with the team and all were taken to the camp. The woman was not seriously hurt, but the four bucks were literally shot to pieces.

I remained several days at the Peninsula, making an excursion into the lava beds in company with Capt. Bancroft of the artillery, and with Bogus Chancy as guide. We explored many of the caves, at least as far as we were able with poor lighting material at our command. I then started to overtake the volunteers, coming up with them before reaching Jacksonville, where Capt. Hizer's company was discharged. Capt. Rogers, of the Douglas county company, was discharged at Roseburg. After this I returned to my newspaper work at Salem, Oregon.

The Indians were moved from Boyles' Camp at the Peninsula to Fort Klamath where five of them, Jack, Sconchin, Black Jim, Hooker Jim and Boston Charley were all executed on the same gallows. One of the murderers of the Peace Commission, "Curley Headed Doctor," committed suicide on the road to Klamath. The remainder of the Indians were then moved to the Indian Territory, where the remnants now live.

Thus ended the farce-tragedy of the Modoc war, a farce so far as misguided enthusiasts and mock humanitarians could make it in extending the olive branch of peace to red-handed murderers. And a tragedy, in that from first to last the war had cost the lives of nearly four hundred men and about five millions of dollars.

The foregoing pages describe in simple language what I saw of the Modoc war. Several so-called histories have been written purporting to be true histories. One by A. B. Meacham in his "Wigwam and Warpath." Meacham wrote with the view of justifying all that Meacham did and said. It was, in fact, written in self defence. Another, by one "Captain Drehan," who claimed to have been "Chief of Scouts." The gallant Captain was simply a monumental romancer. No such man served at any time during the war. Donald McKay was chief of scouts, and the exploits of Drehan existed only in his own imagination. I was personally acquainted with all the officers and know that no such man was there. For the truth of all I have said I simply refer the Doubting Thomases to the official reports on file at Washington.

CHAPTER 15

The Great Bannock War

The last Indian war worthy of mention broke out in the spring of 1877. It was preceded by none of the acts of outlawry which usually are a prelude to savage outbreaks. There were none of the rumblings of the coming storm which are almost invariable accompaniments of these upheavals. Indeed, it came with the suddenness of a great conflagration, and before the scattered settlers of western Idaho and eastern Oregon were aware of danger, from a thousand to twelve hundred plumed and mounted warriors were sweeping the country with the fierceness of a cyclone.

As a rule the young and impatient warriors, thirsting for blood, fame and the property of the white man, to say nothing of scalps, begin to commit acts of outlawry before the plans of older heads are ripe for execution. These acts consist of petty depredations, the stealing of horses, killing of stock, and occasional murder of white men for arms and ammunition. But in the case of the great Shoshone, or Bannock, outbreak, there were none of these signs of the coming storm. Settlers were therefore taken completely by surprise. Many were murdered, their property stolen or destroyed, while others escaped as best they could.

From observation and experience I make the assertion that nine of every ten Indian outbreaks are fomented by the "Medicine" men. These men are at the same time both priest and doctor. They not only ward off the "bad spirits," and cure the sick, but they forecast events. They deal out "good medicine," to ward off the bullets of the white man, and by jugglery and by working upon the superstitions of their followers, impress them with the belief that they possess supernatural powers.

This was especially conspicuous in the Pine Ridge outbreak. The medicine men made their deluded followers believe the white men were all to be killed, that the cattle were to be turned to buffalo and that the red man would again possess the country as their fathers had possessed it in the long ago, and that all the dead and buried warriors were to return to life. This doctrine was preached from the borders of Colorado and the Dakotas to the Pacific, and from British Columbia to the grottoes of the Gila. The doctrine probably had its origin in the ignorant preaching of the religion of the Savoir by honest but ignorant Indian converts. They told their hearers of the death, burial and resurrection of the Son of Man. The medicine men seized upon the idea and preached a new religion and a new future for the red man. Missionaries were sent from tribe to tribe to preach and teach the new doctrine, and everywhere found willing converts.

The craze started in Nevada, among the Shoshones, and in a remarkably short time spread throughout the tribes on both sides of the Rocky Mountains. Lieutenant Strothers of the United States Army and I talked with Piute Indians in Modoc County, after the "ghost dance" scare had subsided, who were firm in the belief that a chief of the Piutes died and then came back. They assured us that they had talked with a man who had seen him, and that there could be no mistake. But they said:

"Maybe so; he did not know. The white man medicine heap too strong for Ingin."

So it was with the Bannocks. Their medicine men taught that the white man was to be destroyed, that his horses, his cattle and his houses and land were to revert to the original owners of the country. Accordingly few houses were burned throughout the raid of several hundred miles. Even the fences around the fields were not destroyed, but were left to serve their purposes when the hated white man should be no more. The few exceptions were where white men were caught in their homes and it was necessary to burn the buildings in order to kill the owners. The home of old man Smith in Happy Valley, on the north side of Stein Mountain, the French ranch in Harney and the Cummins ranch on the John Day were exceptions. In the fights at these places some of the Indians were killed and the houses were burned out of revenge. With characteristic Indian wantonness and wastefulness hundreds of cattle were shot down, only the tongue being taken out for food. They, however, would come back as buffalo and cover the land with plenty. But horses were everywhere taken, and when that armed, mounted and tufted host debouched into Harney Valley they had a mighty herd of from seven to ten thousand horses.

The Bannocks, under their noted chief, Buffalo Horn, left their reservation in Idaho and at once began the work of murder and plunder. Buffalo Horn had served under Howard during a portion of the Nez Perce war, but left him because of his dilatory tactics and his refusal to attack when he had the enemy at his mercy. He told Col. Reddington, who was following Howard as correspondent of the Oregonian and *New York Herald*, that Howard did not know how to fight, that next summer he would fight and show him how to make war.

About the same time, the Shoshones, under Egan and Otis, left their reservation and united their forces in Harney Valley, numbering at that time from a thousand to twelve hundred warriors. They were encumbered, however, by their women and children and a vast herd of stock, and as a result moved slowly. Meantime the scattered detachments of troops were being concentrated and sent in pursuit. But while this was being done the tufted host swept a belt thirty miles wide through western Idaho and eastern Oregon, spreading death and destruction in its path. At Happy Valley they killed old man Smith and his son. Both had escaped with their families to Camp Harney, but had imprudently returned to gather up their horses and bring away a few household effects. Another brother and a young man had accompanied them, but had turned aside to look for stock. The two young men arrived at the ranch after nightfall. It was very dark, and before they were aware of the fact they rode into a herd of horses. But supposing they were animals gathered by the father and brother, rode on. When near the centre a mighty wail smote their ears. Some of the Indians had been killed by the Smiths, and the women were wailing a funeral dirge. One who has never heard that wail cannot imagine its rhythmic terrors.

When the appalling noise broke upon their ears the young man with Smith started to wheel his horse and flee. But Smith caught the bridle reins and whispered to him, "For God's sake don't run," and, holding to the reins, quietly rode out of the herd, the darkness of the night alone proving their salvation.

At the French ranch on Blixen River an attack was made by a detached war party, but Mr. French saved himself and men by cool daring and steady bravery. All were endeavouring to make their escape, French holding the Indians at bay while the others fled along the road. He was the only man armed in the crowd, and at turns in the road would make a stand, checking for a time the savages. The Chinese cook was killed and left where he fell, being horribly mutilated by the Indians. Most of the men with French were in wagons, and only for the bravery displayed by him would certainly have been killed.

About the same time two men were coming out with teams, and hearing of the Indian raid, left their wagons and fled to the Shirk ranch in Catlow Valley. After a few days they returned for their wagons, being accompanied by W. H. Shirk, now a banker at Lakeview, Oregon. The wagons were found as left, and after hitching up the horses, Mr. Shirk rode on ahead, imprudently leaving his rifle in one of the wagons. On the grade above the Blixen ranch Shirk looked back and saw the men coming and had little thought of danger. The men drove up to the crossing, when they were fired upon and both killed. Mr. Shirk was also fired upon, but miraculously escaped death. An Indian on a fleet horse was pursuing him, and his own horse was lagging. As he neared the sage brush toward which he had been making, Mr. Shirk looked back and to his relief saw the Indian off his horse. He thinks the horse fell with the Indian, but they pursued him no farther and he made good his escape. Many other miraculous escapes were made by both men and women, some of the latter escaping almost in their night clothes and on bare-backed horses.

During all this time the scattered forces of the department were being concentrated and sent in pursuit. That indomitable old Scotch hero and Indian fighter, Bernard—who had risen from a government blacksmith to the rank of Colonel of cavalry—who believed that the best way to subdue Indians was to fight and kill them and not to run them to death—was following with four companies of cavalry, numbering 136 men. Behind him was Gen. Howard, with 400 infantry, but with his ox teams and dilatory tactics managed to herd them two days ahead. As the cavalry under Bernard drew near, the Indians called in all detached parties and concentrated their forces. On the 7th of June Pete French joined Bernard with 65 ranchers and cowboys.

Bernard had been ordered by Gen. Howard not to attack, but to wait until he came up. At old Camp Curry, on the western side of Harney Valley, or more properly speaking, on Silver Creek, on the evening of the 7th, Bernard's scouts reported the Indians encamped in the valley, at the Baker ranch, seven miles away. In spite of orders, Bernard, always spoiling for a fight, determined to make the attack at daylight. His four companies numbered 136 men, besides French's volunteers.

Bernard had no confidence in the French contingent and declined to permit them to accompany his command in the attack. He directed French, however, to make a dash for the horse herd and if possible capture the animals, while with his regulars he would charge the main camp. Bernard afterwards, in explanation of his disobedience of orders, claimed that he was misled by his scouts.

Bernard broke camp two hours before daylight, or about two o'clock in the morning. He reached the camp just at break of day. Evidently the Indians were not prepared for him, and "Little Bearskin Dick," one of the chiefs, rode out with a white flag in his hand. Bernard had already made a talk to his men, especially to the recruits, telling them they might as well be killed by the Indians as by him, as he would kill the first man that flinched. As Dick rode up, Bernard spoke to a sergeant and asked him if he was going to "let the black rascal ride over him." Instantly several carbines rang out and "Little Bearskin Dick" for the first time in his life was a "good Indian."

At the same instant the bugle sounded the charge, and the troops bore down upon the encampment, firing their rifles first and then drawing their revolvers and firing as they swept through the great camp. But Bernard had not been fully informed regarding the lay of the camp. After sweeping through he discovered to his dismay that the Indians were encamped on the margin of an impenetrable swamp—in a semi-circle, as it were, and he could go no farther. Nothing dismayed, the column wheeled and rode helter-skelter back the road they had come, this time his men using their sabres. When clear of the camp Bernard turned his attention to the men under Pete French. The latter had gotten into a "hot box," two of his men had been killed and one or two wounded and required help. Bernard was not slow in giving it, and when all were safely joined, Bernard dismounted his men and fought the Indians for several hours with his carbines.

The loss sustained by Bernard in the charge and subsequent engagement was four men killed and several wounded, not counting the loss sustained by French. Bernard continued to hover near the Indians throughout the day. He had taught them a lesson they would not forget. Those terrible troopers on open ground, they discovered, could go where they liked, and that nothing could stop them. Accordingly toward night they withdrew to a rim rock, protected on three sides by high perpendicular walls. The neck of their fort was then fortified and the savages felt they could bid defiance to the fierce troopers. In this fight the Indians lost heavily, forty-two bodies being pulled out of a crevice in the rim rock where they had been concealed. Among this number was Buffalo Horn, the greatest leader of the hostiles.

Toward evening Gen. Howard arrived within seven miles of the hostiles. Bernard sent a courier telling of the position of the Indians and that with reinforcements and howitzers under Howard the surrender could be forced in a few hours, or days at most. They had entrapped themselves, and without water must surrender at the discretion of the soldiers. Gen. Howard, however, complained that his troops were worn out, that he could not come up until the following day, and ended by ordering the command under Bernard to return to his camp. This was Gen. Howard's first fatal blunder, to be followed by others equally as serious. The Indians remained in their position until the next day, when they moved out towards the head of the South Fork of the John Day River. They camped on Buck Mountain three days while Howard was resting his troops. They then moved out leisurely to the north, keeping in the rough mountains to be out of the reach of Bernard's terrible cavalry.

Meanwhile Gen. Howard followed, keeping pace with the Indians. His men were mostly employed in grading roads through the rough, broken country to enable his ox teams to follow. Some have questioned this statement. But I saw with my own eyes the road down Swamp Creek and the mountain road leading down to the South John Day River, seven miles south of the mouth of Murderer's Creek. At the South John Day crossing he again laid over three days while the Indians were resting at the Stewart ranch, seven miles away. Think of an army following a horde of Indians through one of the roughest countries imaginable! No wonder that the fiery Bernard hovered close up to them, ready to strike when opportunity and an excuse for disobeying orders was presented.

Rumours of the coming of the Indians had reached John Day Valley, and my old friend Jim Clark gathered a force of 26 men and started out to discover, if possible, which way the Indians were heading. At Murderer's Creek he ran into them almost before he knew it. They were not the skulking Indians of former years, armed with bows and arrows, but fierce, wild horsemen, armed with modern weapons. In a running fight that followed, a young man named Aldrige was killed and Jim Clark's horse shot from, under him. He escaped into the brush and defended himself so successfully, more than one of the redskins biting the dust, that when night closed in he made his way on foot through the brush to the river and followed the stream all night, wading and swimming it twenty-six times. The balance of his command escaped by outrunning their pursuers and all reached the valley in safety.

As soon as the news spread, the women and children were sent to Canyon City and something over a hundred men gathered at the ranch of a man named Cummins. The latter had seen some service and was elected captain. Some were horseback and others had come in wagons. While the men were making final preparations for starting out in search of Jim Clark, a horseman was seen riding along the side of the mountain to the east of the Cummins ranch. Warren Cassner pointed to the horseman and asked Cummins what it meant.

"Oh, I guess it is a sheep herder," replied the old man.

"A queer looking sheep herder," replied Cassner, and mounting his horse started out to make an investigation.

West of the Cummins house the river was lined with tall cottonwoods which obscured a view of the bald mountain side beyond. As Cassner raised the side of the mountain, enabling him to look over and beyond the cottonwoods, he discovered that the whole mountain side was covered with Indians. Twelve hundred Indians and eight thousand head of horses blackened the side of the slope. He called to the men below to get out. At the same time he saw a party of Indians cutting him off from his men.

Then began a race seldom witnessed in Indian or any other kind of warfare. Men on horseback fled for dear life, while others piled into wagons and followed as fast as teams could travel. But Cummins was a brave man and had a cool head. He succeeded in rallying a half dozen horsemen and at points on the road made such a determined stand that the wagons were enabled to escape. At one point Emil Scheutz was standing by the side of Cummins, when some Indians that had worked around to the side fired a volley, one of the bullets ripping a trench in Scheutz's breast that one could lay his arm into. Scheutz staggered and told Cummins he was shot. The latter helped him to mount his horse and amid a rain of bullets fled for life. That was the last stand. But only for the fact that Bernard had followed the Indians closely, preventing them from scattering, all would have been massacred. As it was most of the men kept running until Canyon City was reached, each imagining the fellow behind an Indian.

At the Cassner ranch many halted and were that evening joined by Col. Bernard with his cavalry. Bernard was told that there were six hundred Umatilla Indians at Fox Valley only a few miles from the John Day River, and knowing that they were only waiting to be joined by the Bannocks, determined to attack the latter before reaching them. He was told that the Bannock's must pass through a canyon to reach Fox Valley. That was his opportunity, and he had sounded "boots and saddles" when Gen. Howard, surrounded by

134

a strong body guard, rode up and ordered him to remain where he was. This was an awful blunder, and cost the lives of a number of settlers in Fox Valley. They, all unconscious of danger, were resting in fancied security when the Bannocks arrived, fraternized with the Umatillas and butchered them in cold blood.

But Gen. Howard had made a still more serious blunder. Gen. Grover was coming into John Day Valley with 400 troops and had reached Prairie City, south of Canyon City, and about 45 miles from the Cummins Ranch. He was coming in ahead of the Indians and would have been in a position, with the troops under Howard, to surround and destroy the savages. He was, however, halted by orders from Howard and turned back to the Malheur Reservation. In justice to Gen. Howard it should be said that he claimed his aide misunderstood the orders, and caused the fatal blunder. But be that as it may, it saved the savages from annihilation or surrender and cost the lives of a large number of citizens throughout eastern Oregon.

From John Day Valley, Gen. Howard continued to herd the savages, following with his ox teams and his army of road makers, while the enemy were sweeping a belt thirty miles in width through the State and spreading death and desolation in their path. Many skirmishes took place before the Indians reached the Umatilla Reservation. Here Gen. Miles encountered them and in the battle that followed completely routed them. Disheartened and losing confidence in the good medicine of their medicine men, the savages split up, a portion going on to Snake River and the Columbia, while the Stein's Mountain and Nevada Piutes doubled on their tracks and started back, for a greater portion of the way over the road they had come. This again left the settlers exposed to butchery and plunder. The military had followed the main bands towards the Columbia and Snake Rivers. One band attempted to cross the Columbia by swimming their stock.

135

A steamer had been despatched up the river armed with Gatling guns and protected by a force of soldiers. While the vast herd of horses and Indians were struggling in the water the boat came in sight and opened with the Gatlings. Some of the Indians succeeded in crossing, but most of them were driven back, and the carcasses of Indians and horses floated down the river.

CHAPTER 16

Snake Uprising in Eastern Oregon

While these events were transpiring all eastern Oregon was wild with excitement. There were no telegraphs through the country in those days, if we except a line running up the Columbia from The Dalles to Pendleton and Walla Walla. The wildest stories were set afloat, which of course lost nothing by repetition.

When the first news of the outbreak reached me I was doing jury duty in Judge L. L. McArthur's Court at The Dalles. I was engaged in the cattle business in what is now Crook County, and my ranch was 95 miles to the south of The Dalles. My family had been left on the ranch which was being cared for by a couple of young men in my employ. My brother, Senator S. G. Thompson also lived a couple of miles from my ranch.

On coming down stairs at the Umatilla House one morning I met Judge McArthur who expressed surprise at finding me yet in town, saying he supposed I and my friends were well on our way home. I replied that I was waiting the good pleasure of the Court.

"Why, man, have you not heard the news?" replied the Judge.

"I have heard no news," I replied, but seeing that the Judge was in earnest asked to what news he referred.

Judge McArthur then told me in a few excited words of

the outbreak of the Bannocks, declaring that in all probability the Indians would reach my section before I could get there.

I waited to hear no more, and running across the street to the livery stable ordered my team harnessed. While I was waiting three young men, one of them being a lawyer named G. W. Barnes, and with whom I had come to The Dalles in a two-seated rig, came up. While the team was being harnessed we secured from a store several hundred rounds of Winchester ammunition, besides a couple of needle guns and some ammunition which we borrowed. One of my friends ran across to the hotel and returned with some provisions for breakfast. We had no time to wait. Other thoughts occupied our minds. We then began the home run, ninety-six miles away. I insisted on driving and nursed the team as best I could, giving them plenty of time on the uphill grade, but sending them along at a furious pace on level ground and downhill. From The Dalles to Shear's bridge on the Deschutes we made a record run. There we changed horses, the generous owner returning not a word when our urgent errand was told. Mrs. Shear also kindly gave us some food to eat on the road. By 1 o'clock we were at Bakeoven, 45 miles from The Dalles. Here we again changed horses, and secured some food, which we literally ate on the run.

Our next lap was a long one and it was necessary to save our horses as much as possible. But we had a good team and made good progress, and when night closed in we were more than 25 miles from home. We finally reached the ranch of old man Crisp, whose son was most savagely butchered a few days later by the Indians at Fox Valley.

My ranch was reached about midnight, possibly a little later, and I found, to my inexpressible relief, that all was well. My wife hastily prepared a cup of coffee for my companions and set them a lunch. While they were eating the young men harnessed up another team, with which Mr. Barnes and companions reached Prineville some time after daylight.

Almost the first word spoken by my wife to me after I had asked the news, was that Capt. George, Chief of the Warm Spring Indians, had been there and enquiring for me. I asked her where he had gone. She replied that he had come there in the evening, and she had ordered supper for him and that he had put up his horse and was sleeping at the barn. The news was a relief to me, you may be sure.

After my friends had gone and while my wife and I were discussing the news, George walked in. He shook hands with me and I gave him a seat. I knew he had news for me. But an Indian always takes his time. After he had sat for some time, and consumed with anxiety to know the nature of his visit, I said:

"Well, George, what is it?"

"Have you heard about the Snakes," was his instant answer.

"Yes, I heard about it at The Dalles, and that was what brought me home. But what do you think about it?"

"I do not believe the Snakes will come this way, but, if they do I will know it in plenty of time. I will then bring lots of Indians over from the reservation, we will gather up your horses, all of Georges' horses and all of Maupin's horses and will take them and all the women and children to the reservation and then we will go out and fight Snakes and steal horses."

That was George's idea of war. It mattered not to him if everybody else was killed, so long as the property and families of his friends were safe. The conversation, of course, was carried on in the Chinook language, which is a mixture of the Wasco tongue and Hudson Bay French.

Captain George was, as I have stated, Chief of the Warm Spring and Wasco Indians. He was one of the most perfect specimens of physical manhood I have ever beheld. He was proud as Lucifer and would scorn to tell a lie. In fact, he was one of the really good live Indians I have known. Years after, when residing at Prineville, my front yard was the favourite camping place of Capt. George, and my stables were always

139

open for the accommodation of his horses. He was my friend, and as he expressed it, "we are chiefs."

Poor old George! He has long since been gathered to his fathers. I do not know that I shall meet George in the happy hunting grounds. But this I know, I will meet no truer friend or braver or nobler soul than that of this brave old Indian.

The next morning after my arrival at home George went up to see my brother, and from there went on to the ranch of Mr. Maupin. So far as I was concerned, after my talk with George, I felt perfectly at ease. I knew he would do as he had promised. But the whole country was in panic and it could not be stayed. Some had abandoned their farms and fled across the mountains to the Willamette Valley, while others were getting ready to go. I allayed the fears of immediate neighbours as far as possible by selecting the ranch of Dr. Baldwin as a rallying point in case of danger. But each hour, almost, would bring a new story of danger and a new cause for a stampede. Some of my neighbours buried their effects and prepared to flee. In the midst of this word reached me one afternoon that the people at Prineville were forting up, and that a company had been organized to go out to meet the Indians. Mounting good horses my brother and I set out for Prineville, nearly thirty miles away. We arrived there about dark after a hard ride, but it did not take me long to size up the situation. The "company" was worse panic stricken than the people, and the fort that had been started was worse than a trap. It was absolutely worthless for defence. Everything, however, was confusion and one scare followed another in rapid succession.

I tried to get a few, men to go with me on a short scouting expedition to discover if the Indians were coming that way. Not one could be found who would volunteer to go. I then returned home and taking one of my young men and a younger brother, struck out for the old Indian trail leading along the crest of the McKay Mountains. After riding some distance, keeping well in the timber, we met two white men who were making their way through the mountains. They told us that the Indians had crossed the John Day at the Cummins ranch, of the fight Jim Clark had at Murderers Creek and the death of young Aldridge. As it was now useless to proceed any further we turned back, and reached Prineville next day. All the ranches were deserted, but we had no difficulty in obtaining food for ourselves and horses.

Chapter 17

Bannocks Double on their Tracks

Matters now settled down, the scare was over and ranchers returned to their homes and began repairing damages. Fences that had been thrown down that stock might help themselves were repaired that as much as possible of the crops might be saved. I returned to my ranch and was busy with haying and harvest when another report reached us, borne on the wings of the wind, that the Bannocks had doubled on their tracks and were scattering death and destruction in their path. The last scare, if possible, was worse than the first. About the same time the Governor ordered Gen. M.V. Brown with the Linn county company, under Capt. Humphrey, to hasten to our aid. This was the only organized troop of the militia available for immediate service, and without loss of time they crossed the Cascade Mountains and arrived at Prineville about the 10th of July.

The company was a magnificent body of men, and represented the best families of Linn County. One of the privates was the son of a former United States Senator, while others were young men of superior attainments—law and medical students. George Chamberlain, present United States Senator from Oregon, was first sergeant of the company, Capt. Humphrey was a veteran of the Civil War, commanding a company in many sanguinary battles. Gen. Brown had seen service during the war between the States, but he, and all were ignorant of Indian warfare. On his arrival at Prineville Gen. Brown sent a courier to my ranch with a letter urging me to join the expedition. My business affairs had been sadly neglected during the past three months, and I was loath to start out on an expedition, the end of which was impossible to foresee. I however went to Prineville and had a consultation with him. Gen. Brown was exceedingly desirous that I should go with him. He called my attention to personal obligations of friendship due from me to him. That settled it and I told him I would go. He authorized me to enlist 15 men as scouts and placed me in command. The number were readily found, they providing their own horses, arms, ammunition and blankets. Provisions were supplied from the commissary.

In Humphrey's company there was a character known as "Warm Spring Johnny," whom I shall have occasion to mention further on. He was transferred to my contingent by order of Gen. Brown, as it was believed he would be of service to me. The start was made from Prineville the next day, our course leading toward the head of Crooked River and the South John Day.

On the evening of the second day we arrived at Watson Springs where we camped for the night. Guards had been placed around the camp and I had laid down on my saddle blanket to rest when Warm Spring Johnny came and sat beside me. He then told me that at this place he saw his first white man. Going into the history of his life—he was then a man about 38 years of age—he told me the Snake Indians had captured him when he was a mere child—so far back that he had no recollections of his parents or of the circumstances of his capture. He was raised by the Snakes, and always supposed he was an Indian like the rest of them, only that his skin was white. He did not attempt to account for this difference—he was an Indian and that was all he knew.

In the spring of 1868, Lieut. Watson arrived and camped at the spring which was forever to bear his name. Here the rim rock circles around the head of the spring in the form a half wheel. Willows had grown up along the edge of the stream that flowed out into the dun sage brush plain. Into this trap Lieut. Watson marched his men and camped. Evidently he felt secure, as no Indians had been seen, besides the Warm Spring scouts were out scouring the country. Probably not a guard or picket was placed about the camp. They had been in camp an hour, and were busily engaged in cooking their meal when from the rim of the bluff on three sides a host of tufted warriors poured a shower of arrows and bullets upon them. Lieut. Watson was killed with several of his men at the first fire, while a number were wounded. The soldiers for protection took to the willows and defended themselves as best they could. But the Snakes had overlooked the Warm Spring scouts, who, hearing the firing, rushed to the rescue and attacking the Snakes in the rear, which was open ground, routed them with the loss of several warriors killed and half a dozen captured.

Among the latter was Warm Spring Johnny. He was taken to the officer who had succeeded Watson in command. Great surprise was expressed at seeing a white man with the Snakes and the soldiers were for making short work of the "white renegade." But it soon became evident that he was as much a wild Indian as any of them, and his youth, about 18, making in his favour he was turned over to the Warm Spring captors to guard, along with the other captives. They were all taken down the little branch a few hundred yards and securely bound and tied to a stunted juniper tree. During the night the Warm Springs indulged in a war dance, each lucky warrior flourishing the scalp he had taken. Along past midnight all the captives excepting Johnny were securely bound to the juniper with green rawhide, a mass of sage brush collected and the captives roasted alive. Johnny told me that every moment he expected to be served in the same manner, and could not understand why his comrades were burned while he was saved. He said he supposed that his skin being white they had reserved him for some particular occasion. I asked him if the soldiers knew that the captives were being burned. He replied that he learned afterwards that the Indians told the soldiers they had all escaped except the white one. The probabilities are that the soldiers were too busy with their own troubles to pay any attention to what was going on in the camp of their allies.

Johnny could speak fairly good English, but to all intents and purposes he was as much of an Indian as any of his copper coloured friends. He was adopted into the Warm Springs tribe and remained with them for a number of years, but marrying a squaw from another tribe moved to the Willamette Valley, where he lived and died an Indian. He was almost invaluable to me because of his knowledge of the ways and signs of the Snakes. But aside from this he was absolutely useless as he was an arrant coward and could not be depended on when danger threatened.

The next day we moved south and after a rapid march reached the Elkins ranch on Grindstone, a tributary of Crooked River. It was known that the Indians were returning practically by the same route they had previously travelled, and our duty was to prevent raids from the main body and protect the property of the settlers as far as was possible.

First gaining permission from Gen. Brown, with my scouts and four volunteers, I started out to discover the camp of the Indians, which from the lay of the country, I thought likely would be at the head of Buck Creek, at a spring in the edge of the timber. About 2 o'clock we arrived at the vicinity of the supposed camp of the Indians, and taking an elevated position, patiently waited for dawn. Finally the gray dawn began to peep over the crest of the eastern mountains, and leading our horses we moved closer. When daylight finally arrived we were within a hundred yards of the spring, but nowhere was there a sign of life.

Assuring ourselves that the renegades had not passed that point, and that they were further back, we started to meet them, meantime keeping a careful lookout ahead. We continued on to Crooked River and despairing of finding or overtaking them, we retraced our steps to camp, arriving there about dark after riding 75 or 80 miles.

The next day it was determined to send a strong detachment into the rough brakes of the South John Day. Accordingly Capt. Humphrey detailed 36 men and I joined him with the scouts. We were absent three days and returned to camp without encountering or seeing any signs of Indians. After resting our horses one day we again struck out, this time going farther north in the direction of Murderers Creek. The country was indescribably rough, and our first night's camp was at the John Day at a point on the trail made by Gen. Howard when he was herding the Indians north. About 10 o'clock one of the men from a picket came in and told me that the Indians were signalling from two sides of the camp. I walked down to where Capt. Humphrey was sleeping and woke him up. We watched the signalling for a few minutes and then sent for Warm Spring Johnny. He said they were signalling that we were a strong party of soldiers and had come from the south. He then explained how the flashes were made. A pile of dry grass was collected and then surrounded by blankets. The grass was then fired and when the blaze was brightest the blankets on one side was quickly raised and again lowered, giving out a bright flash light.

I advised Capt. Humphrey to hold his men in readiness for a daylight attack, feeling certain nothing would be attempted until just at the break of day. We knew, however, they were not far distant and that great care was necessary. After discussing the situation with Capt. Humphrey it was determined to go on as far as Murderers Creek, striking the stream at the Stewart ranch. As we passed over the intervening space we saw abundant evidence of the presence of Indians and proceeded across the bald hills with caution. On the hill overlooking the Stewart ranch we saw quite a commotion, a cloud of dust raising and pointing back towards a deep, rocky, precipitous canyon. Believing the Indians were beating a retreat, we rode forward at the gallop, but arrived only in time to see the last of them disappear in the mouth of the canyon.

On the open ground at the mouth of the canyon we halted. The canyon presented a most forbidding appearance, and to follow an enemy of unknown strength into its gloomy depths was to court disaster. The canyon into which the Indians had been driven was steep, rocky and with the sides covered with brush, while the ridge was covered with scattering pines back to the timber line where rose the jagged, serrated peaks of the extreme summit of the mountain. After taking a careful view of all the surroundings we retreated down the mountain pretty much as we had ascended it.

Capt. Humphrey agreed with me that we did not have men enough to attack the Indians in such a stronghold. There remained nothing but to return to the Stewart ranch and go into camp for the night. While returning we decided to hold the Indians in the canyon if possible and send a courier back to Gen. Brown for reinforcements. Accordingly Ad. Marcks was selected for the night trip. He was familiar with the country and undertook the night ride without hesitation. That night a strong guard was kept around the camp, and daylight came without incident worthy of mention.

It was then decided to circle the canyon into which we had driven the Indians on the previous day. We made the start soon after sun-up, taking a course to the east of the point ascended the day before, and which would enable us to ascend with our horses. We reached the summit of the first steep raise and were rewarded by seeing three scouts disappear in the canyon. We gave chase and fired a few shots from the rifles of the scouts which had no other effect than to cause them to lean a little further forward on their horses and go a little faster. As we passed up the ridge we could see the smoke from the camp fires of the Indians coming out of the canyon. The camp was evidently several hundred yards long and indicated they were in considerable force. Nearing the timber line, the pines became very thick, in fact so dense that we could force our horses through with difficulty. My scouts were a couple of hundred yards in advance, and as we burst out of the brush we came upon the horse herd guarded by four Indians. Taking in the situation at a glance, I put spurs to my horse, and calling to the men to come on, made a dash to cut them off from the canyon down which the herders were endeavouring to force them. We made no attempt to use our rifles, but drawing our revolvers opened fire on the scurrying herders. It was quite a mix-up, but we managed to capture nineteen head of good horses. After the fray I looked around for the first time and discovered that instead of all, but one man had followed me, that was the young boy, Eugene Jones. The others had taken to trees, one going back to hurry up Capt. Humphrey. Had they all followed as did the boy we would have captured every horse and probably have got the herders as well. Descending the ridge on the west side we crossed the trail made by the Indians when coming into the canyon.

At 2 o'clock the next morning I again started to circle the camp with twenty men, leaving Capt. Humphrey at the Stewart ranch. I ascended the mountain farther to the east than the day before and reached the timber line at daylight. A hundred yards or more from the timber line was a clump of stunted trees. I determined to dismount my men and rest our horses. As we were dismounting one of the scouts, Al Igo, asked permission to ride up the ridge a ways and get a better look at the country. I gave consent but cautioned him not to venture too far. As soon as the girths of our saddles were loosened and guards placed around I threw myself on the grass and was asleep in five minutes. But my sleep was of short duration, for Igo came dashing back, calling, "get out of here, we are being surrounded." He said he had counted eighty odd warriors on one side and fifteen on the other.

We lost no time, allow me to assure you, in "getting out of there." A quarter of a mile above us, and about the same distance from the timber line on every side, were three jagged peaks, and not more than twenty yards apart. Here I stationed the men, first dismounting them and securing our horses among the rocks so as to shield them from the bullets of the Indians. I felt sure that we were going to have a fight, and against heavy odds. But the rocks made a splendid fort, and I explained to the men that if they would save their ammunition and not get excited we could stand off all the Indians west of the Rocky mountains. After talking to them I took two men, Charley Long and a young man named Armstrong, two of the best shots in the company, and crawled down through the grass about 150 yards to another pile of rocks. I calculated that if I did not hold that point the Indians could unseen reach it and pour a deadly fire into our position above. Besides I had hopes of getting some of them when they came to the edge of the timber. We had reached the position but a few minutes when two rode out of the timber to our left and about 400 yards away. The boys wanted to fire, but I held them back telling them that we would get surer shots by not disclosing our position. We could see them watching the men in the rocks above, and soon they turned and rode straight towards us, all the while watching the men in the rocks. When within 100, yards I told the men to take deliberate aim and we would fire together. I pulled on the trigger of my needle gun until I could feel it give. But something told me not to fire and I told the men to wait. On they came, and again we drew deadly beads on the unsuspecting horsemen, but there was an indefinable something that told me not to fire. When they had come within thirty yards we discovered they were white men. We rose up out of the rocks and grass and when they came up I discovered that one of them was an old friend, Warren Cassner, from John Day Valley. We also discovered for the first time that the sun was in total eclipse. Everything looked dark, and they had taken us for Indians and we had came within a hairs breadth of sending them into eternity under the same false impression. When I saw how near I had come to killing my friend I was all in a tremble.

The two men belonged to a company of 125 men raised in John Day Valley and Canyon City and were pursuing a large band of Indians that had come in the night before. They made a trail as broad as a wagon road and evidently numbered a hundred or more warriors. Joined with those we had been watching they constituted quite a force and would evidently put up a stiff fight. We returned with the John Day men to the Stewart ranch, and Gen. Brown having arrived during the day, our forces numbered full 250 men, and all full of fight. That night plans were discussed for the coming attack. I favoured dividing our forces and attacking them from both sides of the canyon. In this, however, I was overruled and all was arranged for a combined attack on the Indian position from the west side. It was arranged that I should start at 2 o'clock with 25 men, circle the west side of the camp, and if the Indians had slipped out during the night I was to follow and send back a messenger to the main command. That there might be no mistake as to the course we should take in the morning, I pointed to the canyon in which the Indians were encamped and the ridge up which we would go.

CHAPTER 18

Another Attack that Miscarried

Everything was in readiness. Two hundred rounds of ammunition was distributed to the men, and all were in high
glee at the prospect of being able to revenge the cruel murder
of friends and neighbours.

At 2 o'clock we were roused by the guards. Horses were
quickly saddled and after a meal of bread, meat and coffee
we mounted and filed out of camp. Besides the scouts I had
ten men belonging to the John Day volunteers. As daylight
began to peep over the mountain tops we reached the head
of the canyon in which the Indians were encamped. We had
kept a close lookout for any signs of the Indians abandoning
the canyon but found none. There could be no question as to
their whereabouts—not more than a mile below us.

We halted here and engaged in a discussion as to the advisability of going around to the west side of the canyon, and
when the attack began to open on them from that side. The
John Day men were decidedly in favour of the move. But
Gen. Brown had especially requested that I should be with
the main force when the fight began, and I must return and
meet him. It was finally arranged that I should return, taking
one man with me, while the others should go down the west
side of the canyon. Accordingly I selected the boy Eugene
Jones and we started back. It was arranged that the main force
should follow me up the mountain within an hour after I left

camp, and I expected to meet them about the time the attack began. I did not consider it as being particularly hazardous, as they could not be very far away. We rode at the gallop, expecting every moment to hear the report of the opening guns. It was broad daylight now and we sped on as fast as our horses could carry us. But nothing could be seen or heard of the command. Our situation was now serious in the extreme. We passed within 600 yards of the Indian camp and could see the smoke curling up out of the canyon. But the only alternative that presented itself to us was to go ahead as we should certainly meet the troops within a short distance. As a matter of fact we were "so far stepped in that to retreat were worse than going o'er." On and on we sped until the brow of the mountain was reached overlooking Murderers Creek Valley, and nowhere could we get sight of man or beast. "What does it mean?" These were the questions repeated one with the other. We finally concluded that the Indians had slipped out behind us, or that we had overlooked their trail, and that Gen. Brown finding it had started in pursuit.

Descending the mountain we struck across the valley and at or near the creek we found the trail of the command. It was easy to distinguish the trail as our men rode shod horses while the Indian ponies were bare-footed. Picking up the trail we rode as fast as the condition of our tired horses would permit. About four miles from where we struck the trail we found the carcass of one of our pack mules. We at first thought there had been a skirmish and that the mule had been killed. An examination, however, showed us that the mule had fallen over an embankment and broken his neck. Following a well beaten trail we did not discover that the command had left it until we had gone some two or three miles past the carcass of the dead mule. We therefore began to retrace our steps. It should be understood that the course taken by the command was due east, at right angles to that which they should have taken in following me in the morning. Returning, we carefully examined each side of the trail in order to discover where it had been left. We finally came back to the carcass of the dead mule. We knew they had been there, but what had become of them? Eugene suggested that they had "had an extra big scare and had taken to wing."

While we were looking for the trail six of the men from whom we had separated in the morning rode up. They were as much bewildered as I. In fact, I could not account for the actions of the command except that there was rank, craven cowardice somewhere, and the language I used was freely punctuated with adjectives not fit for print. After a long search we discovered where they had left the trail. They had followed a shell rock ridge for a quarter of a mile, probably, as some of the men suggested, to hide their trail for fear the Indians would follow them. The course was now due north. This they kept until reaching the summit, when they again turned west. We followed on as fast as the jaded condition of our horses would permit, until I discovered pony tracks following behind. Keeping a sharp lookout, however, we continued on until we came to where one of the Indians had dismounted, the imprint of his moccasin being clearly outlined in the dust. This presented a new difficulty, and we now understood why they had not picked us off in the morning. They were entrenched and were waiting to be attacked, but seeing the main force turn tail, the hunted had turned hunters.

To follow the trail further appeared madness, and we turned down the mountain, keeping in the thick cover. I concluded the command would simply circle the camp and return to the Stewart ranch that night. Accordingly we bent our course so as to strike the head of the valley, which we reached at sundown, but nowhere could we discover the presence of man or beast. We waited until dark and then led our horses up through the willows lining the banks of the creek, and finding an open space picketed our horses, and leaving a guard of two men, laid down to sleep. I told the boy Eugene to wake me up and I would stand guard, but he failed to do so, saying he was not as tired as I and stood both guards.

At daylight we again saddled up and began a search for the command. We had eaten nothing since 2 o'clock on the previous morning and began to feel keenly the effects of hunger. All that day we wandered through the mountains, returning to our hiding place in the willows of the night before. At daylight I wrote a note and left it at the Stewart ranch and then determined to reach John Day Valley. Food we must have, and we knew we could find something there. Striking a course through the mountains we reached the Cummins ranch at 4 o'clock that day. We had now been without food for 62 hours, and from that day to this I could never bear to see anything hungry—man or beast. Here we found Gen. Brown with most of his command enjoying their ease. Some kind ladies at the house, learning our condition, quickly set us some food, mostly soups and articles of light diet.

In explanation of his remarkable course, Gen. Brown declared he was misled by the John Day volunteers, while they in turn laid the blame on Gen. Brown. I was furious over the whole shameful affair and took no pains to conceal my disgust. Capt. Humphrey told me that he knew they were going in the wrong direction, and told Brown so, but the latter said Lieut. Angel was acting as guide and that they would follow him, and on the head of that officer the blame finally rested.

This incident and others led next day to the enforced resignation of Lieutenant Angel and the election of George Chamberlain as his successor.

From the Cummins ranch we went to Canyon City for supplies, and from there to Bear Valley, on the mountain to the west, and on the road leading to Camp Harney. After resting our horses for a day, Gen. Brown and I, with a small escort, went to Camp Harney hoping to get some news, and while awaiting the return of Chamberlain. At Camp Harney a small force of regulars was posted and some thirty or forty families had gathered there for protection. Many of the women and children had escaped from their homes, scantily dressed, and had been unable to procure any clothing during the lapse of more than a month. It was a sad sight, especially those who had lost husbands, sons and brothers.

The day after our arrival, two ladies, the wives of Major Downing and Major McGregor, sent for me. The latter had two or three children besides her mother. Their husbands were with Howard's column and they were anxious to reach Canyon City and go from there to Walla Walla. Would I escort them to Canyon City? I said certainly, I would do so, as I would go within a few miles of that place on my return to camp. Lieut. Bonsteil of the regulars spoke up and said he would provide them with an escort at any time. But Mrs. McGregor told him plainly that she would not go with the soldiers that if they got into trouble the soldiers would run away—but the volunteers would stay with them. The Lieutenant suggested that "it was a fine recommendation for the United States Army." "I know the army better than you do, Lieutenant, and have known it much longer, and I will not risk my life and the lives of my children with them," said the plain spoken Scotch lady. The next morning, bright and early, we started out. The ladies were riding in an ambulance, driven by a soldier. When near half way to Bear Valley and near Mountain Springs, we crossed the fresh trail of a strong party of Indians, but we arrived at our destination safely, and next morning returned to camp. Here we rested a couple of days and, Chamberlain returning, we moved to our head camp at Grindstone. We had accomplished nothing in the way of destroying hostiles, but had prevented them from scattering and committing all kinds of atrocities as they had done before reaching John Day Valley.

Arriving at our camp we found ourselves without any provisions. Accordingly Gen. Brown and I started to Prineville with a four horse team to obtain supplies to send back to the men who were to follow. We took along a teamster and the quartermaster. Starting in the evening we arrived at the crossing of Beaver Creek, and I captured an old hen, all that was left at the ranch after its plunder by the Indians in June. We drove until midnight and arriving at Watson Springs, stopped for the night. We dressed the hen and had the driver to sit up the balance of the night and boil her. When daylight came we tried to breakfast off the hen, but it was a rank failure, and we harnessed up and drove on, getting a meal at a ranch ten miles from Prineville, to which place we drove that night.

Thus ended my last Indian campaign, and one of which I never felt any great amount of pride. In one respect it was a rank failure, due, I have always thought, to the rank cowardice of some one—probably more than one. We had, however accomplished some good, as before remarked, and probably saved some lives, and that was worth all the hardships we had endured.

I cannot close this narrative without a further reference to the boy, Eugene Jones. During the first two weeks of the campaign my eyes became badly affected from the dust and glare of the sun, reflected from the white alkali plains on the head of Crooked River. At times I could scarcely bear the light, which seemed fairly to burn my eyeballs. From the first Eugene had attached himself to me. He would insist on taking care of my horse in camp, and often would stop at a spring or stream and wetting a handkerchief would bind it over my eyes and lead my horse for miles at a time. At Murderers Creek, too, he was the only man to follow me when I made the dash after the Indian horse herd. Another thing I observed about the boy was that I never heard him use an oath or a vulgar, coarse expression. What then was my surprise on arriving at Prineville to find a letter from Sheriff Hogan of Douglas County telling me that the boy, Eugene Jones, was none other than Eugene English, a notorious highwayman and stage robber. He was a brother of the English boys, well known as desperate characters. I was stunned, perplexed. The Sheriff asked me to place him under arrest. But how could I do so, after all he had done for me? It appeared in my eyes the depth of ingratitude. In my dilemma I laid the matter before Judge Frank Nichols of Prineville. I related all the boy had done for me, and asked him what, under like circumstances, he would do. "By George, Colonel, I would not give him up. It may be wrong, but I would not do it," replied the old Judge. We then went to Mr. Brayman, a merchant of the town, and laid the matter before him. He fully agreed with us that the boy should be saved. I then went to the quartermaster, got a voucher for the boy's services, obtained the money on the voucher from Mr. Brayman, and putting a man on a horse, explained to him that he was to hand the letter and money to Eugene, first having him to sign the voucher, or warrant, over to Mr. Brayman.

The young man found the boy with the volunteers. He called him to one side, gave him my letter as well as the money. He signed the voucher, and that night disappeared and I never saw or heard of him again. But of this I feel certain, if he fell in with the right class of men he made a good man and citizen. Otherwise, otherwise. Do you blame me, reader? I have never felt a regret for what I did. Put yourself in my place.

CHAPTER 19

Reign of the Vigilantes

Every newly settled country has had to deal, to a greater or less extent, with lawless characters. Generally these outlaws have been brought into subjection and destroyed under the operation of law. Occasionally, however, this, from one cause or another, has been impossible. It is then that citizens, unable longer to bear the outrages committed by desperate criminals, take the law into their own hands and administer justice according to their own ideas of right, and without the forms of law. Such occasions are always to be deplored. They arise from two causes, the maladministration of justice and boldness of criminals whose long immunity from punishment renders them reckless and defiant of both law and the citizens.

Such conditions existed in the late 70s and early 80s in that portion of Eastern Oregon now embraced in the county of Crook. During several years desperate characters had congregated in that section. From petty crimes, such as the stealing of cattle and horses, they resorted to bolder acts, embracing brutal and diabolical murder. For a time the citizens appeared helpless. Men were arrested for crime and the forms of law gone through with. Their associates in crime would go into court, swear them out and then boast of the act. On one occasion I went to one of the best and most substantial citizens of the country, Wayne Claypool, and asked him about an act of larceny of which he had been a witness. He had seen the crime committed from concealment. I asked him if he was going to have the men arrested. He replied that he was not. Then, said I, if you do not I will.

"Mr. Thompson," he replied, "rather than appear against them I will abandon all I have and leave the country. For if they did not kill me they would destroy all I have."

Under these circumstances I was forced to let the matter drop, and content myself with writing an article for the local paper. No names were mentioned and nothing at which an honest man could take offense. Instead of publishing the article as a communication, it was published as an editorial. But scarcely had the paper appeared on the street, than three men, all known to be thieves and desperate characters, caught the editor, knocked him down, pulled out his beard, and would probably have done him greater bodily harm had not Til Glaze interfered and stopped them. While the editor was being beaten he hallowed pitifully, "I didn't do it, Thompson did it." This embittered the whole gang against both Glaze and myself. But they appeared satisfied with threats about what they were going to do, and for the time being made no attempt to carry out their threats against either of us.

This was in the fall of the year. On the 15th of March, 1882, a man dashed into town and riding up to me asked where he would find the Coroner. He was greatly excited and his horse was covered with foam. I told him the nearest officer was at The Dalles, 125 miles away, but that a Justice of the Peace could act in his absence. I then asked him what was the matter? He replied that Langdon and Harrison had killed old man Crook and his son-in-law, Mr. Jorey. I then told him to go to Mr. Powers, the Justice of the Peace. Presently the Deputy Sheriff for that section of Wasco County came to me and asked me to go with him to assist in the arrest of the murderers. There had been some dispute between the murderers and the murdered men, resulting a law suit. It was at best a trivial matter and no further trouble was apprehended.

But immunity from punishment had emboldened the gang and they believed they could do as before, simply defy the law. I declined to go with the Deputy, making as an excuse that I did not feel well. He then summoned me as a posse. I told him to "summons and be d—d," I would not go. That it was a long ride and that the men had been seen "going towards The Dalles, saying they were going to give themselves up." The officer was furious and went away threatening me with the law. But I had other ideas regarding the whereabouts of the murderers.

An old gentleman living on Mill Creek, east of Prineville and about thirty miles from the scene of the murders, had told me of the finding of a cabin concealed in a fir thicket and that it contained both provisions and horse-feed and had the appearance of having been much used, but that there was no trail leading to it. As soon as I learned of the murders I made up my mind that the murderers would go to that cabin. I did not, for reasons of my own, mainly that he talked too much, tell the Deputy of my plans. I went to four men—men of unquestioned courage and discretion—and told them of my plans. These men were Til Glaze, Sam Richardson, G. W. Barns and Charley Long. They all agreed to go with me. It was arranged that we were to slip out of town singly and meet a few miles up the Ochoco Creek, at a designated place. We deemed this essential to success, as we knew that the men had confederates in town who would beat us to the cabin and give the alarm. Meantime the angry Deputy got a posse together and started on his fruitless errand. We loitered about town until about 8 o'clock, taking particular pains to let ourselves be seen, especially about the saloons. We did not talk together, nor did we permit any of the gang to see us in company. We then dropped off saying we were going home, that it was bed time.

But instead of going to bed we mounted our horses and taking back streets slipped out of town. The night was dark and stormy, but all five reached the rendezvous on time and we then proceeded to the ranch of Mr. Johnson whom we requested to pilot us to the secret cabin. The vicinity of the cabin was reached about two o'clock in the morning, and after securing our horses we cautiously approached it. A light was soon discovered and with still greater caution we attempted to surround the cabin.

The barking of a dog, however, gave the alarm and both murderers seized their rifles, blankets and some provisions and made their escape. Jumping over a log behind the cabin they stopped to listen and finally thinking it a false alarm, laid down their guns, etc., and walked around to the corner of the cabin. The snow was a foot deep and so dark was the night that they did not see us until we were within a few feet of them. They then started to run when Richardson, Glaze and Barns opened on them with their revolvers. Long and I were within a few feet of the front door and did not catch even a glimpse of the fleeing murderers. They were chased so closely that they had no time to get either their horses, guns or blankets, but made their escape in the darkness.

When the shooting began the door flew open and a crowd of eleven men made a rush. Long and I were armed with double barrel shot guns, and levelling them on the crowd we ordered them back or we would kill every man of them. You may be sure they lost no time in getting back and closing the door. I then stepped to the side of the door and told them we were after Langdon and Harrison, and did not wish to harm anyone else, but that if one of them stuck his head out of the cabin he would get it blown off.

We had got the horses, blankets and rifles of the murderers, and now began the watch that was to last until daylight. The wind was fierce, even in the shelter of the timber, and a cold snow drifted over us. We had not only to guard the house, but the shed in which the horses were tied as well. Besides, we did not know what would happen when daylight came and they should discover that our party numbered five, instead of twenty, as they supposed. When daylight finally came I went to the door and told those inside to come out and to come out unarmed. They obeyed at once, and eleven men filed out of the cabin. Of the number, there was but one that any of us had ever seen before, or to my knowledge ever saw again. The one was a brother of Langdon, and we at once placed him under arrest that he might not render his brother assistance.

We had agreed on our plans during the night, and taking young Langdon, Long and I started back to town, while the others began to circle for tracks of the fugitives in the snow. I should have stated that when the shooting began the night before, Mr. Johnson mounted his horse and rode home at top speed. Arriving there, he sent one of his sons to Prineville and the other up the Ochoco, telling them that we had the murderers surrounded and were fighting as long as he was in hearing, and were in need of help. Going up the mountain I discovered the tracks of the fugitives in the snow, and as we reached the summit we met 75 or 80 men coming out to help us. I turned them all back, saying the murderers had escaped, and that the rest of our party were coming a short distance behind. I had directed Long to keep by the side of young Langdon and that if he attempted to escape to kill him. I then called out four young men whom I could trust and told them to drop behind and watch for the trail of the fugitives when they should leave the road. We then all returned to Prineville and I turned the young man over to the Deputy Sheriff, telling him to lock him up.

The four young men struck the trail at the foot of the Mill Creek mountain, and following it until convinced the fugitives were endeavouring to reach home to get horses, abandoned it and struck out through the mountains the nearest route to the Langdon place. They reached the ranch just as the men had got horses and some food and were coming through the gate. Five—even one minute and they would have been too late. But levelling their shot guns on the murderers they surrendered. They were then brought to town, and instead of awakening the officers, they came to my house and asked me to get up and take charge of the prisoners. This circumstance enabled my enemies, especially the outlaw gang, to accuse me of being the head of the vigilantes. The prisoners were held at the livery stable, and as soon as I arrived I sent for the Deputy Sheriff and City Marshal, and on their arrival moved the prisoners to the bar room of the hotel. The Deputy asked me to remain and assist in guarding the prisoners.

At the hotel the Deputy and Marshal guarded the street door, while I kept watch on the back door. Langdon was shackled and laid down on a lounge and fell asleep. Harrison was sitting near me and had started in to tell me all about the murder. I was sitting sidewise to the street door, and hearing it open, turned my head just as four men sprang upon the two officers and bore them to the floor. At the same instant two men rushed across the room and levelled their revolvers at me. The whole proceedings did not occupy five seconds, so sudden was the rush. All were masked, even their hands being covered with gloves, with the fingers cut off.

In another instant the room was filled with the uncanny figures. Apparently every man had a place assigned him, and in less time than one could think, every entrance to the hotel bar room was guarded by armed men. As the two men levelled their guns at me I put up my hands, and I want to say I stood at "attention." At the same time two men ran around the bar room stove, and as Langdon sprang to his feet one of them struck him with his pistol. The weapon was discharged and they then emptied their revolvers into his body. While this was going on other men placed a rope around the neck of Harrison and as he was rushed past me he wailed, "For God's sake save my life and I will tell it all." But I saw no more of him until next morning, when he was hanging under the bridge that spanned Crooked River.

Twelve men were left in the room after the main mob had gone. Not a word was spoken until I asked permission to go to the body of Langdon and straighten it out. Both men bowed, but followed me closely, at no time taking either their eyes or revolvers off me. They were, however, very cool, and I felt little danger of an accidental discharge of their weapons. After about twenty minutes one of the figures gave a signal and in an instant all were gone, passing out through two doors.

It was now nearly daylight and a great crowd gathered about the hotel. There was a great deal of suppressed excitement, but I cautioned all to be prudent and not add to it by unguarded language. The mob appeared to be thoroughly organized, every man having and occupying his assigned place. This fact gave Harvey Scott an opportunity to declare in the Oregonian that I "was the chief of the vigilantes, and could have any man in three counties hanged" that I should order.

Matters now quieted down for a time and it was hoped that no more such disgraceful scenes would darken the fair name of our citizens. As time wore on the gang again became more bold and many acts of outlawry were committed. Sometime in December a stock association was organized, with a constitution and by-laws. It was agreed that no one should ride the range without notifying the association. Copies of the by-laws were sent to every stock owner in the county and all were asked to join.

Along in January, about the 10th, as I remember, a crowd of the rustlers came to town, and after filling up with bad whisky rode up and down the streets, pistols in hand, and declared they could take the town and burn it, and would do so "if there was any monkey business." Little attention was paid to them, people going about their business, apparently unconcerned. But that night there was "monkey business." Three of the gang were hung to a juniper two miles above town, while another was shot and killed in town. The next morning notices were found posted, with skull and crossbones attached, telling all hard characters to leave the county. There was then such a *hegira* as has seldom been witnessed. Men not before suspicioned skipped the country. They stood not upon the order of their going, but went—and went in a hurry. Among the number was an ex-Justice of the Peace.

Again things quieted down. The county was divided, courts organized and justice administered without let or hindrance. The reign of the vigilantes was over, and citizens everywhere looked to the law for protection.

Chapter 20

The Passing of the Mogans

A few years previous to the occurrences before given, two young men arrived in the county and gave their names as Tom and Frank Page, being brothers. I gave one of them, Frank, employment on my cattle ranch, but soon became satisfied that he was not the right kind of a man, and discharged him. Both remained in the section, accepting such employment as they could obtain. One day a man came along and recognized the Page brothers as men he had known in Nevada under a different name. Hearing of this, they admitted that the name first given was an alias, and that their true names were Mike and Frank Mogan. They were a quarrelsome pair and posed as bad men, and were not long in involving themselves in trouble and were shunned by the better class of citizens. In a case against the younger of the two, Frank Mogan, a young lawyer, C. W. Barnes, was employed as opposite counsel. This seemed to embitter both men against Barnes and some threats were made against him. No attention was paid to the matter by Barnes, but he kept a watch on them when in their company.

Finally in the fall after the last lynching Mike came to town and in order to pick a quarrel with Mr. Barnes, began to abuse his younger brother, a boy of about 17 years. The boy went to his brother and told him of Mogan's conduct. He was told that if he associated with such men as Mogan he must suffer the consequences. The boy then went home, and securing an old cap and ball revolver, came back to the street. Mogan began on him again, and after suffering his abuse for some time, drew the revolver and shot him through the chest. Mogan ran a short distance and drawing his revolver, started back. Seeing that young Barnes was ready for him, he turned off, walked a short distance, sank down and died the next day. The affair created some excitement. The boy was arrested but subsequently came clear.

At the time of the homicide I was out of town and knew nothing of the shooting until late that night. The other Mogan brother, however, affected to believe that I had given the revolver to the boy and had told him to use it. I explained to him the absurdity of the charge, proving to him that I was out of town. This appeared to make no difference, he still holding a grudge against me for discharging him. He made many threats against my life, all of which were borne to me. He declared he would "kill me if he had to lay behind a sage brush and shoot me in the back." Still I paid no apparent attention to the threats, being satisfied he would never at any rate face me.

One evening I was called to the store of Hahne & Fried to attend to some business. It was just after dark and while I was there I was notified by a friend that a daughter of Judge Nichols had overheard Mogan tell one of his friends that he had come to town to kill me and would not leave until he had accomplished his purpose. This was going a little too far, and I determined to settle the matter one way, or the other at our first meeting. The test came sooner than I anticipated. On seeing me he attempted to draw his gun but was too slow, and fell with more than one bullet: through his body.

I sent for Sheriff Geo. Churchill and surrendered myself as a prisoner. He told me to go home and if he wanted me he would send me word. The committing magistrate, at my request, placed me under bonds to appear before the Grand

Jury. The announcement caused an uproar among the throng with which the court-room was packed, and I was compelled to go among them and explain that it was done at my especial request. I wanted the matter to come up in the Grand jury room and so told the people. The Oregonian published distorted and untruthful statements regarding the affair, and attorneys from every part of the State volunteered their services to defend me free of charge. I wrote to them, of course thanking them, but told them I had no use for attorneys, as the matter would never go beyond the Grand jury, and there it ended, the District Attorney, Mr. McBride, proving my strongest witness.

I have gone somewhat into detail in this matter through no spirit of bravado, for no one could deplore the necessity of my action more than I. But to show to those who have never experienced frontier life the dangers, difficulties and hardships through which one must pass. It may be said that I should have had Mogan arrested for threatening my life. To such I will say that under all the circumstances such a course would only have still more embittered the situation and made the end inevitable. Another thing, among frontiersmen the man who goes to law for protection of that kind, makes of himself a pusillanimous object for every vagabond to spit upon and kick. I was not "built: that way."

CHAPTER 21

The Lookout Lynching

Coming down to a later date, perhaps no event of its character has attracted so much comment, and been the subject, of more gross misrepresentation than the "Lookout Lynching." I have, therefore, been asked to give a true account of the deplorable affair, the causes leading up to the same, and the sensational trial of nineteen citizens accused of participating in the act.

To begin at the beginning: Along in the early 70s the United State government established a military post at Fort Crook, in Fall River valley, which was occupied by a company of cavalry under command of one Capt. Wagner. The post was designed to afford protection to settlers against depredations by hostile Indians. Soon after the arrival of the troops the Captain began to cast eyes of favour on a comely young Indian woman, the wife of a Pit River brave. The Captain had been sent to civilize the Indians, and was not long in taking the woman under his protection. The arrangement was agreeable to the woman, who preferred the favour of the white chief to that of her dusky husband.

Time wore on and the government concluded to abandon the post, and ordered Capt. Wagner and his company elsewhere. Of course, he could not take the Indian woman with him, and she must be got rid of. The means presented itself in the person of a soldier named Calvin Hall, whose term of enlistment had expired. He proposed to Hall that if he would take the woman off his hands he, the Captain, would give him a small portable sawmill which the government had sent to the post to saw lumber with which to build quarters, etc. The arrangement being agreeable to Hall, the trade was made and the woman and sawmill passed to a different ownership.

In the course of time Hall sold the sawmill and settled on a piece of land not far from the present town of Lookout. Here the two full blood children of the woman grew to manhood. Another child was born to the woman, the father being a man named Wilson, with whom she lived during one of her changes of lovers, for Mary (her Christian name) was a woman of many loves. The half breed boy was fifteen years old, and probably by reason of environment was not a model. The two full bloods, Frank and Jim Hall, the names by which they were known, gradually became looked upon as desperate characters. Their many misdeeds brought them into prominence, and frequent arrests followed. But somehow Hall managed to enable them to escape the vengeance of the law. This only served to make them bolder in their misdeeds. Cattle were killed and horses mutilated, merely because the owners had incurred their enmity. The school house in the neighbourhood was broken open, books destroyed and other vandal acts committed. In fact, they became the terror of the neighbourhood, the Hall home being a place of refuge and shelter, and Hall a protector when arrests followed their crimes.

This condition of affairs could not exist for long. When the law fails to protect life and property, I have always observed that men find a way to protect them. About a year and a half before the finale, a gentleman living in Lookout visited Alturas and detailed the many misdeeds of these men to me. One in particular I remember. Dr. Shearer, a wealthy stock man living some distance this side of Lookout, had employed some Indians in harvesting his hay crop. Frank Hall had a grievance against the Indians, and during their absence from their camp went there and cut their wagons and harness to pieces. The Indians trailed him to within a short distance of Halls, but were afraid to go further. They complained to Mr. Shearer, who promptly sent word to Frank Hall that if he ever came on his ranch he, Shearer, would shoot him. Sometime after this Mr. Shearer found a saddle animal belonging to his wife cut and mutilated in a most shameful manner. The horse, a beautiful animal and a pet, had his ears and tail cut off, while deep gashes were cut in his side and hips. Mr. Shearer could not prove that Frank Hall committed the dastardly act, but was more than satisfied of his guilt. This and other like acts were detailed to me, and I wrote an article for my paper detailing the grievances of the people of that section and ending by predicting that, unless it was stopped, "juniper trees would bear fruit." My prediction came true a year and a half later, only that the Pit River bridge and not the junipers bore the fruit.

Sometime during the year of 1900 a man named Yantes came to the vicinity of Lookout and took up with the Halls. Later he took Mary, the Indian woman, away from old man Hall, and lived with her on a ranch he had located. He carried a big gun and posed as a bad man, and of course found genial companionship in the sons of the Indian woman. The coming of Yantes seemed to add to the boldness and reckless conduct of Frank and Jim Hall and the half-breed boy Wilson. Along towards the last of May, 1901, a burglary was committed in the neighbourhood. Of course the Hall crowd was suspected and a search warrant obtained. At the Hall home several of the articles were found, as well as on the persons of the men. The hides and meat of animals recently killed were found at the Hall and Yantes homes and the brands identified by the owner. This discovery led to the arrest of the entire gang, including Hall and the half-breed boy Wilson. They were taken to Lookout and a guard placed over them.

The Grand jury was in session at Alturas, and next morning R. E. Leventon and Isom Eades came to Alturas to secure the indictment of the men. The proof was positive, and they felt that at last a conviction could be secured. But unfortunately the Grand jury adjourned that morning. They then applied to the District Attorney to go to Lookout and prosecute the criminals. But Mr. Bonner had a case coming up at Lake City, and the Justice refusing to postpone it, could not go. The matter was finally arranged by the appointment by Mr. Bonner of C. C. Auble, an Adin attorney, as a special deputy to prosecute the cases. The appointment was made out and given to Leventon and Eades, but Mr. Bonner, a young lawyer and serving his first, term, made the fatal mistake of instructing Mr. Auble to dismiss the charge of burglary and re-arrest the men for petty larceny.

During all this time the five men, two white men, the half-breed boy and the two Indians, were held under guard, the bar room of the hotel being used for the purpose. When it became known that the prisoners were merely to be prosecuted for the smaller crime, the whole country became aroused. Both Yantes and the Halls made threats of dire vengeance upon those instrumental in their arrest. They declared they would get even as soon as they were free. All knew the Indians and Yantes to be desperate men, and to turn them loose would be equivalent to applying the torch to their homes, if not the knife to their throats. Accordingly at the hour of 1:30 on the morning of May 31st a rush was made by masked men, the prisoners taken from the guards and all five hung to the railing of the Pit River bridge.

The news spread like wildfire and created intense excitement throughout the county and State. The great papers, in two column headlines, told of the "wiping out of a whole family."

"An old man," said they, "his three sons and his son-in-law," were ruthlessly hung for a petty crime, the stealing of a few straps of leather. In Modoc county the sentiment of nine-tenths of the people was that the leaders of the mob should be punished. Young Banner had made a mistake, due doubtless to youth and inexperience, but it remained for Superior Judge Harrington to make a still more serious one.

Judge Harrington wrote to the Attorney-General asking that detectives and a special prosecutor be sent to investigate and prosecute the case against the lynchers. He also called the Grand jury together in special session. But there never was any evidence.

The Grand jury convened on June 10th, and a host of witnesses were in attendance.

The result of the Grand Jury session was the returning of indictments against R. E. Leventon, Isom Eades and James Brown. As the case against Brown appeared to be the best, he was "brought to trial" November 21, 1901. Assistant Attorney-General Post and Deputy Attorney George Sturtevant were sent from the Attorney-General's office to prosecute the case. The prisoner was defended by ex-Judge G. F. Harris, E.V. Spencer and John E. Raker.

Soon after the trial began Judge Post sent for a noted gunfighter named Danny Miller. And during all those weary three months of the trial he could be seen trotting around after Post, his moustache turned up, a la William of Germany, like a rat terrier following a mastiff, to the infinite amusement of the small boy and utter disgust of sensible men. Gibson, the noted San Francisco detective, was here, assisted by other detectives and a dozen or more local head hunters, who were after a share of the big reward. District Attorney Bonner was pushed aside and completely ignored. He was not even given an insight into what was going on. In justice to Mr. Sturtevant I want to say that he had no hand in the high-handed measures adopted by Post and Harrington. And had he been in control the result of the Brown trial might have ended differently. Indeed, so favourably were the people of Modoc impressed with Mr. Sturtevant that members of both parties—prominent citizens—went to him and offered him the Superior Judgeship at the coming fall election. For reasons of his own he declined, and before the end of the Brown trial left in disgust.

At one stage of the proceedings there was talk of supplying troops from the National Guard to preserve order. And yet there had at no time been a breach of the peace or threats made except by the man Miller. On one occasion Miller drew a revolver in the court room and attempted to shoot Attorney Raker. At another time he beat a young man named Russell over the head with a gun for some fancied offense. A brother of young Russell kept the principal hotel in the town, and both had been open in their denunciation of the lynchers. I mention these facts to show why it was that the citizens of the county turned from nine-tenths in favour of prosecuting the lynchers to the utmost limit, to nine-tenths the other way.

Early in January Detective Gibson went to a young man who was stranded in Alturas with his wife and offered him a portion of the reward, amounting to $900, to testify to a certain matter. The young man and his wife were working, for their board, but he told Gibson that he knew nothing of the matter and that poor as he was he would not swear to a falsehood. Gibson went away, but returned a few nights, later and again tried to get him to testify, saying that the men were guilty and that no one would ever be the wiser. Slavin (the young man's name) then told Gibson that if he ever came to his home with such a proposal that he, Slavin, would shoot him like a dog. All these attempts at bribery soon became known and filled citizens everywhere with consternation. They argued that under such methods an innocent man might be sacrificed that a lot of head hunters could gain a big reward.

On January 4th, 1902, Mary Lorenz, a half breed daughter of old Mary Hall, swore to a warrant charging, fifteen others with complicity in the lynching. All were arrested, but not one was found to be armed. They were placed in jail, and on the 10th indictments were filed charging each one with five different murders.

The causes leading to these arrests were said to be the confessions of John Hutton and Claude Morris.

It subsequently developed that Morris was taken to a room, there plied with whisky by the detectives, aided by Simmons, and at two o'clock in the morning signed an affidavit that had been prepared for him. After he regained consciousness he denied the whole thing, but was told that he would be sent to the penitentiary for perjury if he went back on the confession he had signed before a notary public. Under the circumstances the poor, weak boy, kept under guard and away from friends and relatives, was compelled to stick to the evidence that had been prepared for him.

As the trial of Brown dragged its "slimy length along," the scenes in the court room at times beggared description. Harrington, badgered by the attorneys for the defence, raved like a madman, and generally ended by sending one or more of the attorneys for Brown to jail. He refused to permit any evidence to be introduced for the purpose of impeachment. Disinterested men were brought from Tule Lake to prove that the boy Hutton was on his way to Lookout from that place when the lynching took place. Another witness was placed on the stand and testified that he stood on the ground, back of Leventon's shop and saw certain of the accused, among them Brown, and heard them plotting. Harrington refused to permit any evidence to be introduced tending to impeach the witness.

When Harrington would rule against the admission of this evidence, Harris, Raker or Spencer would argue the point and manage to get the evidence before the jury and end by going to jail. The attorneys took turns going to jail, but managed for one to remain outside to conduct the case. Thus wore away the weary months until the jury brought in a verdict of "not guilty." In conversation with one of the jurymen that morning he stated that the character of the witnesses for the prosecution was enough. They were Indians, half-breeds, and disreputable characters of every shade and degree.

The morning after the verdict was rendered not one of these creatures could be found. During the night they had fled and scattered like a covey of quail. They feared arrest for perjury, of which they were guilty. All that remained the next morning was General Post and his gun man, Danny Miller. They took the stage after breakfast and were seen no more. The prisoners were discharged one and two and three at a time and quietly returned to their homes.

Thus ended the dreary farce of the prosecution of the Lookout lynchers. It had cost the county about $40,000 and had accomplished nothing, save to blacken the character of our citizens and cause the outside world to look upon us as outlaws and desperadoes.

Conclusion

The events here recorded were seen with my own eyes, or were received from the lips of the actors therein. Hundreds of men and boys passed through equal or greater dangers and privations than I, and are entitled to equal or greater credit. Reared in the wilderness and on the frontier of civilization, I was merely the product of environment, and lay claim to no particular distinction above those who were my companions. And yet, as I look back over the past, I must be excused for a feeling of pride in having been a part, however insignificant, in the building here on the western rim of the continent, of the mighty Empire of the Pacific.

To have seen proud cities rear their heads from a wilderness—from a cluster of log huts in a primeval forest—whose everlasting stillness was alone broken by the yells of savage men, the long howl of the wolf and the scream of the panther—is something to have lived for.

And yet I question if those who now possess this land of plenty—this land of "milk and honey" ever give a thought for those who "Conquered the Wilderness" and made it a fit and safe abode for the millions of civilized men and women who now enjoy its blessings.

LEONAUR

ALSO FROM LEONAUR

AVAILABLE IN SOFTCOVER OR HARDCOVER WITH DUST JACKET

CAMP-FIRE AND COTTON-FIELD *by Thomas W. Knox*—A New York Herald Correspondent's View of the American Civil War.

SERGEANT STILLWELL *by Leander Stillwell*—The Experiences of a Union Army Soldier of the 61st Illinois Infantry During the American Civil War.

STONEWALL'S CANNONEER *by Edward A. Moore*—Experiences with the Rockbridge Artillery, Confederate Army of Northern Virginia, During the American Civil War.

CONFEDERATE BLOCKADE RUNNER *by John Wilkinson*—The Personal Recollections of an Officer of the Confederate Navy.

THE SIXTH CORPS *by George Stevens*—The Army of the Potomac, Union Army, During the American Civil War.

THE RAILROAD RAIDERS *by William Pittenger*—An Ohio Volunteers Recollections of the Andrews Raid to Disrupt the Confederate Railroad in Georgia During the American Civil War.

CITIZEN SOLDIER *by John Beatty*—An Account of the American Civil War by a Union Infantry Officer of Ohio Volunteers Who Became a Brigadier General.

COX: PERSONAL RECOLLECTIONS OF THE CIVIL WAR--VOLUME 1 *by Jacob Dolson Cox*—West Virginia, Kanawha Valley, Gauley Bridge, Cotton Mountain, South Mountain, Antietam, the Morgan Raid & the East Tennessee Campaign.

COX: PERSONAL RECOLLECTIONS OF THE CIVIL WAR--VOLUME 2 *by Jacob Dolson Cox*—Siege of Knoxville, East Tennessee, Atlanta Campaign, the Nashville Campaign & the North Carolina Campaign.

THE RELUCTANT REBEL *by William G. Stevenson*—A young Kentuckian's experiences in the Confederate Infantry & Cavalry during the American Civil War.

KERSHAW'S BRIGADE VOLUME 1 by *D. Augustus Dickert*—Manassas, Seven Pines, Sharpsburg (Antietam), Fredricksburg, Chancellorsville, Gettysburg, Chickamauga, Chattanooga, Fort Sanders & Bean Station.

KERSHAW'S BRIGADE VOLUME 2 by *D. Augustus Dickert*—At the wilderness, Cold Harbour, Petersburg, The Shenandoah Valley and Cedar Creek.

www.ingramcontent.com/pod-product-compliance
Lightning Source LLC
Chambersburg PA
CBHW021103090426
42738CB00006B/488